Little
black book of
CBT

CRISTINA POPA, PCC

VELDHOVEN 2022

C PROJECT

For general information on our other products and services or to obtain technical support, please contact us on **www.cproject.nl** or reach out to the author at cris@cproject.nl

C Project publishes it's books in a variety of electronic and print formats. Some content that appears in print might not be available in electronic form and vice versa.

C Project is not associated with any product or vendor mentioned in this work.

Little black book of CBT

Interior and Cover Designer: Jan-Joost Molemans

Art Producer: Luana Mangione

Editor: Giuseppe De Mattia

Production Editor: Sophie Bosma

Production Manager: Joaquim Montaner

All ilustrations used under license from iStock

@Cproject.nl   Client artwork

Contents

Foreword

This book is a gift for all readers who are open to the possibility of personal growth and change. Among the most exciting and impactful innovations in the field of mental health over the past several decades has been the development of short-term forms of psychotherapy that are pragmatic, goal oriented and well-studied. Of all these evidence based therapies, CBT sits atop as the broadest and most impressive.

The skills and principles of CBT are now applied widely to help treat diagnosable disorders like social anxiety, depression, posttraumatic stress disorder, obsessive compulsive disorder, eating disorders and substance use disorders. But the benefits of CBT extend well beyond the realm of clinical diagnoses. CBT has also proven useful for a wide range of common human problems such as stress, strained relationships, anger, procrastination and low self-esteem, just to name a few of the important topics this workbook touches on. Elements of CBT are increasingly incorporated into education and training programs in schools and workplaces because of their documented efficacy and far-reaching value for improving our everyday quality of life. Light on jargon and replete with wisdom and valuable exercises, The Little Black Book of CBT promises to become the to-go resource for individuals interested in pursuing CBT on their own or who wish to incorporate this book as homework with a skilled therapist.

As a psychiatrist who has often prescribed reading or bibliotherapy to patients (and myself!) it's a joy to discover this remarkable workbook. I expect this workbook will be used carefully and returned to frequently- even by initially skeptical readers and those currently burdened by challenges that make routine tasks a chore. The author clearly understands and empathize with the challenges we all face. She neither patronize us nor let us off the hook easily. She furnish a trove of inventive, useful and feasible exercises, each introduced by a concise statement of principles and objectives. Much like musicians and athletes, readers who practice these exercises – perhaps tentatively and reluctantly at first – will find their CBT muscles growing steadily stronger. For many readers, what starts off as thoughtful tips and interesting exercises will likely get incorporated as novel frameworks for thinking and behaving and developing positive habits for more healthy lives.

On behalf of all of us who know that life is not always easy, my admiring thanks to the author who has given us a wealth of actionable insights and steps to support us on our journey.

Anna Bartoccini MD, PCC

Senior Fellow MD and Professor of Psychiatry
Istitutto di Formazione Cognitivo-Comportamentale
Centro di Psicologia Clinica, Pescara, Italy

This little black book
belongs to

____

____

If you found this, please call

____

____

Introduction

Welcome to the **Little black book of CBT**. If you're reading this, you might be looking for ways to improve your state of well being. You are not alone. Everyone experiences barriers that block them from being where they would like to be emotionally, mentally and even socially.

This workbook allows you to GET OUT OF PERFECTIONISM, SELF-SABOTAGE and identify what are your barriers, explore where they are rooted and begin to respond to them by refraiming your thoughts, emotions and behaviours.

In becoming aware and more mindful of your thoughts in this way, you will find that you feel more confident in yourself and you behave in a way that sustains healthy relationships with yourself and others.

This workbook is based on Cognitive Behavioral Therapy. Cognitive behavioral therapy is a short-term, skill-based psychotherapy treatment that helps people learn to assert more influence over their thoughts, behaviors, and feelings to effectively solve life's challenges.

CBT teaches us a philosophy of life that can be learned by everyone in order to be happier. The ideas and philosophies in CBT stem from ancient and modern philosophers, science, psychology, common sense and humanity. The results obtained following the CBT approach are supported by a wealth of research and used extensively by majority of psychologists, coaches and menthal health professionals

Cognitive behavioral therapy, or CBT for short, is a treatment that helps people build skills to effectively handle the challenges that life throws at them.

Overwhelming research over the past two decades has shown CBT to be the most effective therapy for a whole host of problems: anxiety, depression, OCD, anger, phobias, eating disorders, substance abuse, assertiveness, shame, avoidance, procrastination and relationship problems, just to name a few.

Because CBT teaches people to solve their own problems by learning and practicing new skills, CBT helps people stay well long after treatment is complete.

How Cognitive Behavioral Therapy (CBT) works?

To appreciate how CBT works, it will be helpful to understand the core components of the CBT model:

1. Situations themselves are generally not problematic. It is our reactions to situations that cause problems. This may seem counter-intuitive, because when something goes wrong, we usually point to the thing in our environment that started it all. But in most situations, it's the way we handle the challenge that dictates whether/to what degree the situation becomes a problem. Take the example of not getting the job you wanted. For some people, this could serve as a devastating blow in their careers, causing them to avoid putting themselves out there again and instead just settle for the jobs they have. For others, it may feel temporarily disappointing, but they're able to use that disappointment to assess what (if anything) went wrong, and bolster their training and experience to make themselves more marketable next time. It's not the situation, but the reaction that really counts.

2. Thoughts play an outsize role in how we experience the world and how we feel. Similar to the component discussed above, life events alone don't dictate our experience of the world; the thoughts we have about life events are what shape our experience. Technically, thoughts mediate the relationships between situations, moods, and behavior. This means when something doesn't go our way, it's the way we think about the situation that determines whether it's a permanent setback or merely a challenge to be solved. For instance, when we wave to someone we know on the street and they don't wave back, our habitual way of making sense of things takes over. If we're prone to self-defeating thoughts, we might think "They're ignoring me because they don't like me. They don't want anything to do with someone like me." This line of thinking might lead us to avoid the person and eventually lose contact with them, resulting in a kind of self-fulfilling prophecy. If we're in the habit of having thoughts grounded in our actual experience, we might think "They probably didn't see me," and not have even a second thought about the event.

3. Our behavior also affects how we think and feel. It's not just that when we have certain thoughts we act a certain way. The converse is true too; when we act a certain way, our behavior affects how we think about situations. An example is avoiding situations we don't look forward to, for instance, avoiding talking to strangers at parties.

When we avoid socializing because we're uncomfortable, our thoughts tend to fill in the blanks of our experience about what socializing is like. We might have thoughts that "talking to strangers is too uncomfortable," or "I'm no good at talking to people," "I won't have anything to say," or "They won't like me if they get to know me."

The problem is, if we continue to avoid socializing, we aren't really giving ourselves the opportunity to collect evidence to the contrary, so our self-defeating thoughts are reinforced. We end up believing them even more and engage in even more avoidance.

4. Our thoughts, feelings, and behavior are constantly influencing each other. These components are interrelated. A change in one changes the others as well. Not only do thoughts shape moods, but moods can shape thoughts. When we feel a strong emotion for whatever reason, our thoughts tend to fall in line with that emotion. Take for example, drinking a double-shot of espresso on your day off. You might have been looking forward to all the things you were going to do today, but consuming too much caffeine can trigger physiological anxiety, and you may notice your thoughts take a more fretful tone. The more anxious we feel, the more likely we are to avoid things we otherwise wouldn't, and pretty soon the day is ruined. All of these components are constantly influencing one another.

5. Changing thoughts, behavior, or feelings results in changes in the other components. The good news is, we can use this system to our advantage. If we've been feeling depressed, small changes in thoughts/behavior can set off a chain reaction to feeling better. The more we tweak thoughts and behavior, the more we wrestle back influence over our mood. This is what we teach people to do in CBT, make small changes in thoughts and behavior to effect big changes in feelings.

Understanding this model of emotions can help you think about problems differently and can illuminate new ways of making positive changes in your life. All of the exercises in this online CBT workbook are designed to teach you these underlying mechanics of your mind so you can feel better and achieve your goals.

Will CBT Work For You?

A lot of factors influence how effective CBT is for different people, but the one that matters most is the level of effort you put into practicing the skills.

Like any new skill, it may feel difficult at first, and if you don't practice regularly, it might always seem difficult. The intention of cognitive behavioral therapy is to help you rehearse the skills so often that you don't need to think about skills when a challenge arises. You just do what needs to be done spontaneously. With this in mind, it's important to be diligent about completing the exercises as many times as you need to gain mastery of the techniques.

Other factors that predict whether people succeed in CBT are how ingrained the problem is, and how severe the problem is. If you have been struggling with depression for a decade, it will take more time and effort to treat than if you have felt depressed for only a month. Similarly, if your depression has you not getting out of bed for a week at a time, rather than just feeling a little down most days, you'll probably need more help.

Although many people can benefit from using the self-help techniques in this workbook on their own, if you think you may have a psychiatric disorder, it's highly likely that you'll benefit most from working with a cognitive behavioral therapist.

Much of the positive research focused on CBT has examined people who are completing CBT exercises at home while working with a trained CBT therapist. If you've been suffering for a long while or your symptoms feel very intense, you owe it to yourself to consider pursuing CBT therapy with an experienced CBT therapist. No workbook can compare to working with a trained mental health professional.

The Cognitive Behavioural Model

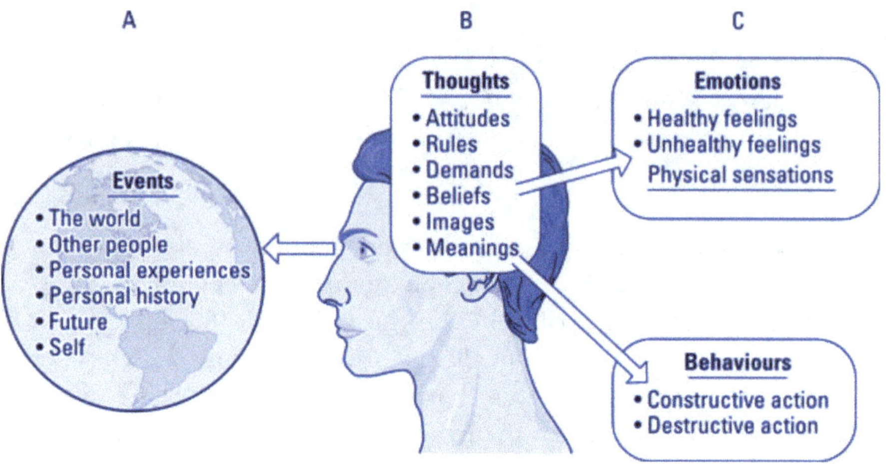

Thoughts / Beliefs

What a person thinks or believes about a situation. How the individual interprets an event

Situation

Anything that happens to a person. Situations are ultimately outside of the individual's control, but they can be influenced by behaviours.

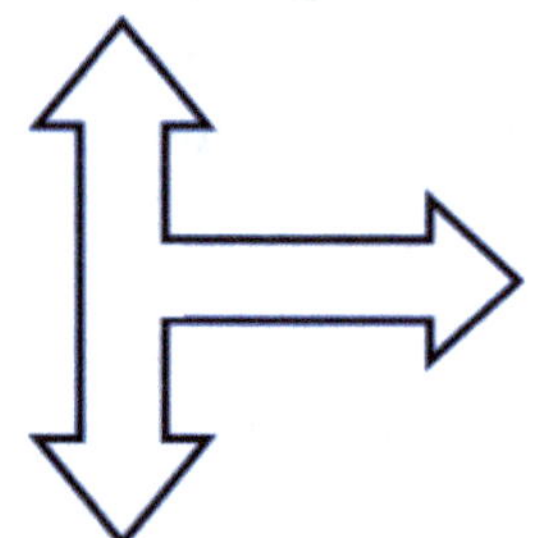

Behaviour/ Response

The person's action and behaviours in response to their thoughts and feelings about a situation.

Emotions

How a person feels about a situation. Emotions are not neccessarily based in logic, but they are influenced by thoughts and beliefs.

The Cognitive Model

Thoughts   Emotions   Behaviors

Cognitive behavioral therapy is based on the idea that how you think determines how you feel and how you behave. The diagram and example below show us this process:

Something happens. It could be anything.	You have **thoughts** about what has just occurred.	You experience **emotions** based upon your thoughts	You respond to your thoughts and feelings with **behaviors.**

Example: John
Situation: A stranger scowls at Joe while passing him on the street.
Johns Thoughts: *"I must've done something wrong… I'm so awkward."*
John's Emotions: Embarrassed and upset with himself.
John's Behaviors: John apologizes to the stranger and replays the situation over and over in his head, trying to understand what he did wrong.

In this example, you might've noticed that John's thought wasn't very rational. The stranger could've been scowling for any number of reasons. Maybe the stranger just got dumped, or maybe he scowls at everyone. Who knows?
As humans, we all have **irrational thoughts** like these. Unfortunately, irrational or not, these thoughts still affect how we feel, and how we behave. Consider how John might've responded to the same situation if he had a different thought:

Thought  Emotion  Behavior

Thought	Emotion	Behavior
What a jerk!"	Angry	John shouts: "What's your problem?!"
He must be having a bad day…"	Neutral	John walks away and forgets the incident.

Using the cognitive model, you will learn to identify your own patterns of thoughts, emotions, and behaviors. You'll come to understand how your thoughts shape how you feel, and how they impact your life in significant ways.

Once you become aware of your own irrational thoughts, you will learn to change them.

The thoughts that once led to depression, anxiety, and anger will be replaced with new, healthy alternatives. Finally, you will be in control of how you feel.

How to use this workbook

This workbook is organized to help you learn and practice the skills that are foundational to CBT so you can apply them to whatever problems come your way. It's organized in such a way that most people will find it easiest to start at the beginning, slowly and repeatedly applying the exercises in each module, and only moving to the next module once they feel they have mastered the previous one.

The best way to use this workbook is to take it one section at at time.

Part one assesses your current mental health state. It gives you space to define goals, values and areas that need improvement.

Part two identifies the negative self-talk and thoughts you're having, where they stem from and how to reframe them.

Part three looks at your behaviours and how they are affecting your relationship.

Part four focuses on moving forward managing your emotions, coping with stressors and performing self-care. It is best to tackle the sections in order as they build upon each other.

Part five looks at how to prevent relapse and assure the continuation of the progress achieved so far

Part six is providing supporting materials not specifically discussed in the previous chapters

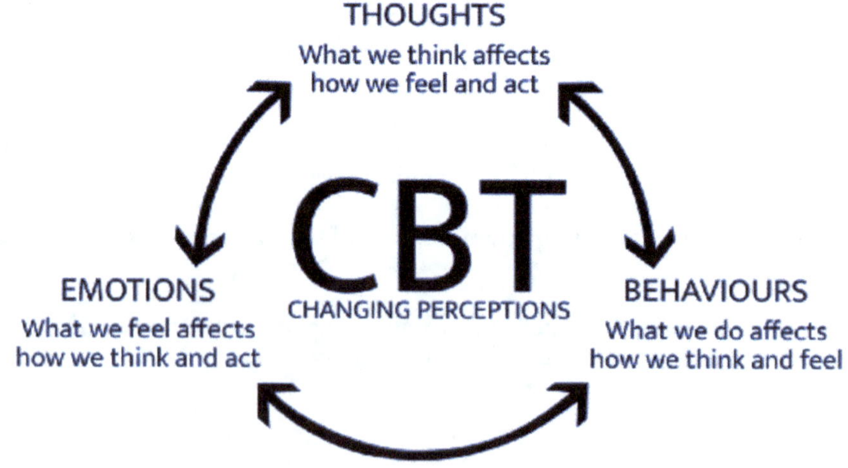

PART ONE: Awareness

The first step is to develop a specific, concrete understanding of what you would like to change. This may be trickier than it sounds, because we're used to viewing our problems subjectively and sometimes vaguely—for example, you might have a general feeling of discontent, or say, "I'm unhappy" or "I can't seem to get it together."

When we view our problems subjectively, it's as if we're sitting inside the problem and can't see outside of it. As you use this workbook to help make changes, you will move toward a more objective view of your experience and of problems. Viewing the problem from a distance, you'll be able to see it more clearly.

Defining your problems objectively will help you start to make this change. With an objective perspective, you're working with the facts, not how good or bad something feels.

Use the following guide and worksheets to develop an objective understanding of the issues that you would like to address.

- Window of tolerance: what is your current state of mind? Are you mentally ready for self-reflection ?

- General Issues identification: identify what are the issues you would like to work
on and describe the problem you would like to work on

- Understand and challenge your own cognitive distortions

- Mindfulness is a cognitive behavioral therapy exercise that helps people disengage from harmful ruminating or obsessing, learning to connect to the present moment.

This first part should take you between 1 - 2 months to complete. It's recommended that you don't go to the next section until you have masteres the awareness phase and understand and accept the issues you want to work on actively

WHAT IS
THE WINDOW OF TOLERANCE?

Most people can deal with the demands and stress of everyday life without much difficulty. However, for those who have experienced trauma, anxiety, or other mental illness, it can be difficult to stay in your optimal zone. Recognizing your window of tolerance and what happens to you physically and emotionally is an important first step. This knowledge enables you to widen your window of tolerance and improve that optimal zone.

How Trauma Can Affect Your Window of Tolerance

When the balance is interfered with, either due to trauma or extreme stress, we end up leaving our window of tolerance. Our bodies typically react defensively to this.

This is where you will begin to dysregulate and experience fight or flight responses. If it is not possible to fight or flee, your body will collapse to the freeze state.

When the body responds defensively, it is just trying to keep us safe. This is a normal response when you are put in unsafe situations. However, trauma and extreme stress can create these similar responses that stick with us, even long after the event has passed.

Any undue stress or anxiety generates fear and negativity that could result in your body triggering those defenses. This is because your mind thinks the trauma or extreme stress you experienced in the past is reoccurring.

WINDOW OF TOLERANCE

The window of tolerance and different states that affect you

HYPERAROUSAL

- Abnormal state of increased responsiveness
- Feeling anxious, angry and out of control
- You may experience wanting to fight or run away

DYSREGULATION

- When you start to deviate outside your window of tolerance you start to feel agitated, anxious, or angry
- You do not feel comfortable but you are not out of control yet

SHRINK
your Window
of Tolerance

Stress and trauma can cause your window of tolerance to shrink

Meditation, listening to music, or engaging in hobbies can expand your window of tolerance

EXPAND
your Window
of Tolerance

DYSREGULATION

- You start to feel overwhelmed, your body might start shutting down and you could lose track of time
- You don't feel comfortable but you are not out of control yet

HYPOAROUSAL

- Abnormal state of decreased responsiveness
- Feeling emotional numbness, exhaustion, and depression
- You may experience your body shutting down or freeze

WINDOW OF TOLERANCE AWARENESS WORKSHEET

Identify, recognize the symptoms you experience and build awareness

For HYPERAROUSAL, check all the symptoms you experience and enter the level of severity from 1 to 5 (one is the least severe and five is extreme and paralyzing):

- Abnormal state of increased responsiveness
- Feeling anxious, angry and out of control
- You may experience wanting to fight or run away

HYPERAROUSAL

○ ___ Anxiety	○ ___ Addictions
○ ___ Impulsivity	○ ___ Over-Eating
○ ___ Intense Reactions	○ ___ Obsessive Thoughts/Behaviour
○ ___ Lack of Emotional Safety	○ ___ Emotional Outbursts
○ ___ Hyper-Vigilance	○ ___ Chaotic Responses
○ ___ Intrusive Imagery	○ ___ Defensiveness
○ ___ Tension	○ ___ Racing Thoughts
○ ___ Shaking	○ ___ Anger/Rage
○ ___ Rigidness	○ ___ Physical and Emotional Aggression
○ ___ ------------------------------	○ ___ ------------------------------
○ ___ ------------------------------	○ ___ ------------------------------

For HYPOAROUSAL, check all the symptoms you experience and enter the level of severity from 1 to 5 (one is the least severe and five is extreme and paralyzing):

- Abnormal state of decreased responsiveness
- Feeling emotional numbness, exhaustion, and depression
- You may experience your body shutting down or freeze

HYPOAROUSAL

○ ___ The feeling of being disconnected	○ ___ Decreased Reactions
○ ___ No Display of Emotions	○ ___ Shame/Embarrassment
○ ___ Auto-Pilot Responses	○ ___ Depression
○ ___ Memory Loss	○ ___ Difficulty Engaging Coping Resources
○ ___ Feign Death Response	○ ___ Low Levels of Energy
○ ___ Numbness	○ ___ Can't Defend Oneself
○ ___ Disabled Cognitive Processing	○ ___ Shutdown
○ ___ Reduced Physical Movement	○ ___ Can't Say No
○ ___ ------------------------------	○ ___ ------------------------------
○ ___ ------------------------------	○ ___ ------------------------------

Tips for smooth sailing within your window of tolerance

You can try any of these techniques to support you when you feel you're leaving your window of tolerance. Using these strategies as a regular practice, even when you're not triggered, can also help to widen your window.

Mindfulness. Stay in the here and now. Notice how you're feeling in response to certain stimuli. What's stressing you out most days? What memories are popping up? Tuning into yourself – with curiosity rather than criticism – can gradually help you become aware of your triggers. Knowing your triggers is the first step to managing them, rather than acting from them.

Breathing. Deep breathing from your belly can help ground you and bring you back to yourself if you feel you're being triggered. Try breathing in through the nose for a count of 5, then breathing out through the mouth for a count of 5. Do this for a few minutes. The longer out-breath will help to calm you.

Physical activity. Moving around can help shift your energy and regulate your arousal levels. If you're more prone to hyper-arousal then some vigorous physical activity may help you to purge some of   the anger or overwhelm you're experiencing. From a hype-aroused state, some gently stimulating exercises – such as rocking yourself –may help you bring you back to yourself.

Soothe your senses. Think about things to look at, touch, smell, hear and taste. What soothes you in the moment will be unique to each individual. You may want to listen to calming music, light a scented candle, look through old photos of beautiful scenery, make your favourite food, or soothe yourself with a blanket. Find what works for you.

Challenge your thoughts. If you're able to catch a negative thought, try to challenge it with a more positive one. Imagine what a good friend would say to you. Try to hear that kinder voice in your head to balance out any negative critical thoughts.

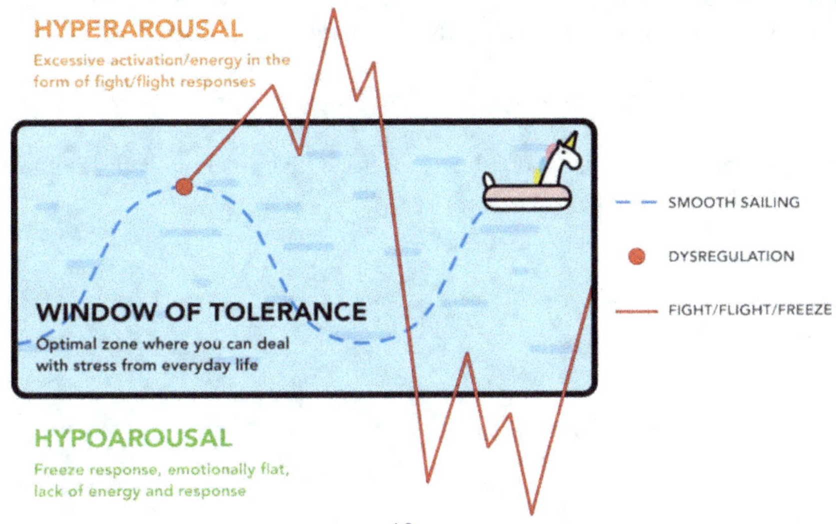

General issue identification

Step one: Start with identifying general issues. What has been bothering you? Some examples might be low mood or depression, low self-esteem, shame, anxiety or excessive worrying, low productivity or difficulty getting things done, anger, habits you want to change like smoking or drinking, or difficulty asserting yourself.

 You might also be struggling with things that are not on this list. Really, any problem you're having or anything you'd like to change is fair game for CBT.

As you learned in the previus pages, it's our reactions to situations that tend to cause problems, rather than the situations themselves. If you find that your issues are external events or situations, like losing a job or breaking up with a romantic partner, try to think about how that event has impacted you. For example, losing a job might lead to sadness and low mood, depending on the thoughts you have about it.

Step two: For each general issue, describe what that problem looks like in your life. Be specific. Many issues can look different for different people.

For example, if you go to a doctor for treatment of a strange pain, you probably wouldn't say, "My problem is that I'm in pain" and leave it at that. You'd explain where you feel the pain, how strongly you feel it, when it first started, whether it is stronger at certain times of the day, and whether anything you do makes it worse or better. You might also describe how the pain feels—is it sharp and stabbing or dull and throbbing? When you feel it, does it come and go in waves or is it consistent? Here, you'll go through a similar process of describing the issue as if you were helping someone else understand exactly what is going on.

Are there certain thoughts, actions, and emotions that go along with the issues you identified?

General Issues Worksheet- EXAMPLE

Instructions: In the General Issues box, list all the general issues you'd like to work on. Then for every general issue you identified, describe what the problem looks like in more detail using the next boxes, filling out one box for each issue. Fill out as many pages as you need.

General Issues:
lack of assertiveness, low self-esteem

#1 (issue:lack of assertiveness)

Specific Description of Issue (issue:________________________________)
I have trouble expressing my opinions to friends and at work. I think that I have to agree with everything my friends say or they'll be angry with me. At work, I don't speak up during meetings because I worry that I don't know the right things to say. I'm afraid to ask anyone out on a date because I'm sure they would say no.

Thoughts: I don't know what to say, I'm not qualified to be here, I always say the wrong things

Emotions: Fear, anxiety, worry

Actions: Going along with what other people say and do, hiding my own views

---

Specific Description of Issue (issue: #2 low self-esteem)
I don't think that I'm worth as much as other people. I don't like myself and I don't think other people really like me either. I think people are just trying to make me feel better when they pay me compliments or say I did a good job on something.

Thoughts: I'm useless, I'm not as good as other people, why bother trying? I won't do well.

Emotions: shame, sadness, hopelessness

Actions: Not trying as hard as I could, pulling away from other people, isolating myself

General Issues Worksheet

Instructions: In the General Issues box, list all the general issues you'd like to work on. Then for every general issue you identified, describe what the problem looks like in more detail using the next boxes, filling out one box for each issue. Fill out as many pages as you need.

General Issues:

____
____
____
____

Specific Description of Issue (issue:_______________________________)

____
____
____

Thoughts:____

____

Emotions:____

____

Actions:____

____

Specific Description of Issue (issue:_______________________________)

____
____
____

Thoughts:____

____

Emotions:____

____

Actions:____

____

General Issues Worksheet

Instructions: In the General Issues box, list all the general issues you'd like to work on. Then for every general issue you identified, describe what the problem looks like in more detail using the next boxes, filling out one box for each issue. Fill out as many pages as you need.

General Issues:

____
____
____
____

Specific Description of Issue (issue:_______________________)

____
____
____

*Thoughts:*_______________________________
____

*Emotions:*_______________________________
____

*Actions:*_______________________________
____

Specific Description of Issue (issue:_______________________)

____
____
____

*Thoughts:*_______________________________
____

*Emotions:*_______________________________
____

*Actions:*_______________________________
____

General Issues Worksheet

Instructions: In the General Issues box, list all the general issues you'd like to work on. Then for every general issue you identified, describe what the problem looks like in more detail using the next boxes, filling out one box for each issue. Fill out as many pages as you need.

General Issues:

Specific Description of Issue (issue:________________________)

Thoughts:

Emotions:

Actions:

Specific Description of Issue (issue:________________________)

Thoughts:

Emotions:

Actions:

General Issues Worksheet

Instructions: In the General Issues box, list all the general issues you'd like to work on. Then for every general issue you identified, describe what the problem looks like in more detail using the next boxes, filling out one box for each issue. Fill out as many pages as you need.

General Issues:

____
____
____
____

Specific Description of Issue (issue:_______________________________)

____
____
____

*Thoughts:*____
____

*Emotions:*____
____

*Actions:*____
____

Specific Description of Issue (issue:_______________________________)

____
____
____

*Thoughts:*____
____

*Emotions:*____
____

*Actions:*____
____

What are Cognitive Distortions?

"I have the worst luck in the entire world." "I just failed that math test. I'm no good at school, and I might as well quit." "She's late. It's raining. She has hydroplaned and her car is upside down in a ditch."

These are all prime examples of cognitive distortions: thought patterns that cause people to view reality in inaccurate — usually negative — ways.

In short, they're habitual errors in thinking. When you're experiencing a cognitive distortion, the way you interpret events is usually negatively biased.

Most people experience cognitive distortions from time to time. But if they're reinforced often enough, they can increase anxiety, deepen depression, cause relationship difficulties, and lead to a host of other complications. Below some distortions explained

Polarized thinking: habitually think in extremes. When you're convinced that you're either destined for success or doomed to failure, that the people in your life are either angelic or evil, you're probably engaging in polarized thinking.

Catastrophizing: to dread or assume the worst when faced with the unknown. When people catastrophize, ordinary worries can quickly escalate. For instance, an expected check doesn't arrive in the mail. A person who catastrophizes may begin to fear it will never arrive, and that as a consequence it won't be possible to pay rent and the whole family will be evicted.

Personalization One of the most common errors in thinking is taking things personally when they're not connected to or caused by you at all. You may be engaging in personalization when you blame yourself for circumstances that aren't your fault, or are beyond your control.

Mental filtering: Another distorted thought pattern is the tendency to ignore positives and focus exclusively on negatives. Interpreting circumstances using a negative mental filter is not only inaccurate, it can worsen anxiety and depression symptoms. Researchers found that having a negative perspective of yourself and your future can cause feelings of hopelessness. These thoughts may become extreme enough to trigger suicidal thoughts.

Labeling is a cognitive distortion in which people reduce themselves or other people to a single — usually negative — characteristic or descriptor, like "drunk" or "failure." When people label, they define themselves and others based on a single event or behavior.

Mind reading: When people assume they know what others are thinking, they're resorting to mind reading. It can be hard to distinguish between mind reading and empathy — the ability to perceive and understand what others may be feeling. To tell the difference between the two, it might be helpful to consider all the evidence, not just the evidence that confirms your suspicions or beliefs.

15 COGNITIVE DISTORTIONS

15 common Cognitive Distortions that influence your thinking patterns

1. POLARIZED THINKING

When you have an "All-or-Nothing," or "Black and White" thinking pattern. Desire to be perfect or you are a complete failure.

2. MENTAL FILTERING

NEGATIVE MENTAL FILTERING

Focuses on negatives of a situation and filters out positives. Negative details are magnified.

DISQUALIFYING THE POSITIVE

Acknowledges positives but refuses to accept it. Finds excuses to turn it into a negative one.

3. OVERGENERALIZATION

Focuses on a single event and makes a conclusion based on a single piece of negative evidence. Incorrectly conclude all similar events going forward will result in the same negative experience.

4. JUMPING TO CONCLUSIONS

MIND READING

Know what others are thinking. Assumptions of their intentions occur with no evidence.

FORTUNE TELLING

Make conclusions and predictions with no evidence and can have negative outcomes.

5. CATASTROPHIZING

MAGNIFICATION

Over exaggeration, which leads to worries escalating to the worst-case scenario.

MINIMIZATION

Minimizing positive experiences. The importance of positive qualities is diminished.

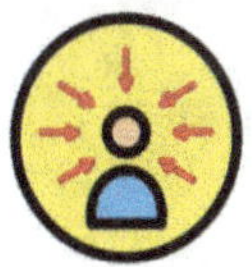

6. PERSONALIZATION

Takes things personally, which causes a direct and personal reaction to what others do or say, even if it is unrelated. Assuming you have been intentionally excluded or targeted.

7. BLAMING

Blaming others, playing a victim role, and holding others responsible for their pain. Blame is external rather than blaming themselves or taking some responsibility.

15 COGNITIVE DISTORTIONS

15 common Cognitive Distortions that influence your thinking patterns

8. LABELING

Assign judgment to yourself or others based on one negative incident. Instead of recognizing you or others made a mistake, you attach a label that is exaggerated and solely based on the single incident.

9. ALWAYS BEING RIGHT

Always have the need to be right. Internalize opinions as facts and will put others on trial to prove their opinions or actions are correct. Will go to great lengths to demonstrate their belief.

10. SHOULD STATEMENTS

"Should" do, "must" do, or "shouldn't" do statements are enforced on themselves or others. These rules create a lot of pressure, imposing a set of expectations that is not likely to be met.

11. EMOTIONAL REASONING

Any feeling must be true in their mind. The emotion is accepted as fact because all logical reasoning is blocked out. Incorrectly assumes the negative feeling is the only truth.

12. CONTROL FALLACIES

EXTERNAL CONTROL FALLACY
Life is completely controlled by external factors. Creates a feeling of no control of the situation.

INTERNAL CONTROL FALLACY
Has control of themselves and their surroundings. Responsible for the pain & happiness of others.

13. FALLACY OF CHANGE

Others should change to suit your interests. Pressure others to change because you feel the change will bring happiness. Convinced the happiness is dependent on the person changing.

14. FALLACY OF FAIRNESS

All things in life should be based on fairness and equality. In reality, not all things work out the way we expect them to, which leads to feelings of anger and resentment towards those things in life.

15. HEAVEN'S REWARD FALLACY

Rewarded based on how hard you work. Will be disappointed because most things in reality are not fair. This leads to feelings of frustration, anger, and resentment.

CHALLENGE COGNITIVE DISTORTIONS

How to challenge 15 common cognitive distortions with examples of reframed thoughts

1. POLARIZED THINKING

CHALLENGE:
- Avoid thinking in extremes
- Don't choose either/or extremes
- Identify how to be less extreme and more flexible
- Think in shades of gray
- Find the middle ground

EXAMPLE THOUGHT:
I received an A- on an exam when I am typically used to receiving A+ grades only, I feel like a failure.

REFRAMED THOUGHT:
I didn't do as well on the exam as I had hoped. But an A- is still a really good grade and I am grateful for it.

2. MENTAL FILTERING

NEGATIVE MENTAL FILTERING

CHALLENGE:
- Don't dwell on a single negative
- Focus on all positives that occurred during the situation
- Reflect on the entire situation
- Identify both positive & negative aspects

EXAMPLE THOUGHT:
I received my employee performance review, but I can't stop thinking about one negative comment my manager made about me.

REFRAMED THOUGHT:
I was lacking in one area of my review, but I performed well in other aspects of my job, and my manager did praise me for a great work ethic.

DISQUALIFYING THE POSITIVE

CHALLENGE:
- Value positive aspects as much as negative ones
- Take pride in accomplishments
- Embrace compliments or positive feedback
- Cultivate an attitude of gratitude

EXAMPLE THOUGHT:
I received a good mark on my assignment, but it's probably a mistake. I'm pretty sure it was just luck or fluke, I don't normally get good grades.

REFRAMED THOUGHT:
I received a good mark on my assignment. I am grateful to receive this grade and am proud of what I accomplished.

3. OVERGENERALIZATION

CHALLENGE:
- Believe you can create different outcomes in the future
- Reflect when a single negative had a long-lasting impact
- Identify evidence that suggests it will impact future events

EXAMPLE THOUGHT:
I failed this exam, I feel like such a failure. I don't think I am smart enough to take this class, I will probably just fail it.

REFRAMED THOUGHT:
I didn't pass this one exam, but in the past, I have always found a way to come back from a failed exam. I will work harder and try again the next time.

CHALLENGE COGNITIVE DISTORTIONS

How to challenge 15 common cognitive distortions with examples of reframed thoughts

4. JUMPING TO CONCLUSIONS

MIND READING

CHALLENGE:

• Ask yourself if you are sure you actually know what someone is thinking

• Investigate your assumptions

• Identify logical reasons that contributed to the situation

EXAMPLE THOUGHT:

I visit a friend, but her expression towards me seems negative. She doesn't want to see me. She claims she was sick, but I feel like she is avoiding me.

REFRAMED THOUGHT:

She could be really sick and wants rest. Other reasons why she wouldn't want to see me: self-conscious about her appearance or worried she is contagious.

FORTUNE TELLING

CHALLENGE:

• Ask yourself how do you know what will actually happen

• Is there evidence to suggests it

• How often have you been accurate in the past

EXAMPLE THOUGHT:

I'm going to have a bad day today.

REFRAMED THOUGHT:

Today may have some challenges, but I will overcome them and have a good day.

5. CATASTROPHIZING

MAGNIFICATION

CHALLENGE:

• Take the negative event for what it is

• Don't make it any more than it is

• Look for opportunities rather than the catastrophic event

EXAMPLE THOUGHT:

There is a lot of traffic on my way to work, I'm never going to get there on time.

REFRAMED THOUGHT:

I may be late, but I will get there safely, in the meantime, I can enjoy the radio.

MINIMIZATION

CHALLENGE:

• Take positives for what it is

• Try not to diminish the importance of positive qualities and turn it into a negative

• Embrace positive experiences & take pride in accomplishments

EXAMPLE THOUGHT:

As an athlete, I win an award, but it doesn't seem like I accomplished much as others have already won this award.

REFRAMED THOUGHT:

I won an award, I am proud of what I accomplished and grateful for how far I have come in my athletic career.

6. PERSONALIZATION

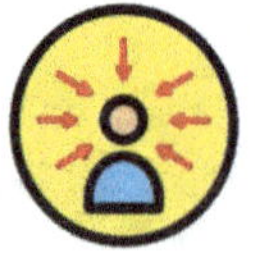

CHALLENGE:

• Identify why you feel responsible

• Determine if you were in control

• Acknowledge it is rarely one person's fault

• Brainstorm logical reasons rather than blaming yourself

EXAMPLE THOUGHT:

My partner and I show up late to a dinner party. Everyone seemed mad and not having a good time because we showed up late. I Should have left earlier.

REFRAMED THOUGHT:

Even though we were late, I cannot control how people feel. There could be other factors that contributed to people not enjoying the party before arriving.

CHALLENGE COGNITIVE DISTORTIONS

How to challenge 15 common cognitive distortions with examples of reframed thoughts

7. BLAMING

CHALLENGE:
- Avoid playing victim role
- See from other's perspective
- Recognize blame does not always fall on one person
- Take responsibility for your role
- Identify solutions and move on

EXAMPLE THOUGHT:
I blame my significant other for the relationship issues we experienced. Why am I always treated this way, only if they put more effort into our relationship.

REFRAMED THOUGHT:
A relationship takes two people to make it work. I am equally responsible for the issues we may have. I should apologize for my mistakes and move forward.

8. LABELING

CHALLENGE:
- Remember labels are the result of an error or mistake
- Attribute the error to the event instead of yourself or others
- One failure does not define you, separate this from labels

EXAMPLE THOUGHT:
Someone at work made a mistake that had severe consequences for other tasks. Why are people so stupid, now I have to redo everything.

REFRAMED THOUGHT:
I understand mistakes can happen. I will spend extra effort to fix it, but it's not the end of the world. I know they are capable of doing a better job next time.

9. ALWAYS BEING RIGHT

CHALLENGE:
- It is acceptable to be wrong
- Mistakes are allowed to happen
- Be open-minded to other's suggestion
- Try and identify if your thoughts are facts or opinions

EXAMPLE THOUGHT:
I didn't agree with the way a task was being performed. I told them how to do it, I don't know why they won't listen to me. It should be done my way.

REFRAMED THOUGHT:
I don't really know which method is better until I try it for myself. Maybe we can go with their method this time and see how it works out.

10. SHOULD STATEMENTS

CHALLENGE:
- Identify how it makes you feel
- These statements should be motivating rather than conflicting
- Use the word prefer in place of should

EXAMPLE THOUGHT:
I should stop being lazy and exercise today.

REFRAMED THOUGHT:
I would prefer to exercise today. But I'm not feeling up for it today. If I don't exercise today, I can exercise the next day.

11. EMOTIONAL REASONING

CHALLENGE:
- Let yourself feel emotions
- Be mindful without judgement
- Avoid letting emotions become truths
- Challenge the validity of feelings and identify if it is based on facts

EXAMPLE THOUGHT:
I feel alone and uncared for because my partner does not want to spend time with me and instead is working overtime.

REFRAMED THOUGHT:
My partner is working overtime because they are busy at work. Not because they do not care for me. When they are not busy they spend time with me.

CHALLENGE COGNITIVE DISTORTIONS

How to challenge 15 common cognitive distortions with examples of reframed thoughts

12. CONTROL FALLACIES

EXTERNAL CONTROL FALLACY

CHALLENGE:

• Look for opportunities in small changes before big ones

• Recognize you cannot control everything

• Identify things in your control and things out of your control

EXAMPLE THOUGHT:

I feel overwhelmed and anxious due to the coronavirus pandemic. I feel like I have no control to protect myself or my family from the virus.

REFRAMED THOUGHT:

I recognize I cannot control how the virus spreads but I can reduce the risks by protecting myself, such as face masks and washing my hands regularly.

INTERNAL CONTROL FALLACY

CHALLENGE:

• Recognize you can't control everything around you

• Think whether your actions actually contributed to it

• Is there someone else that needs to take responsibility

EXAMPLE THOUGHT:

My daughter failed her exam. I blame myself because I think I should have spent more time helping her study.

REFRAMED THOUGHT:

Maybe she failed her exam because it was really difficult, not because I am a bad parent. I can offer to help, but it is her decision to put more effort.

13. FALLACY OF CHANGE

CHALLENGE:

• Recognize no one is responsible for your own happiness

• Separate the change from your own happiness

• Your happiness depends on yourself and the actions you take

EXAMPLE THOUGHT:

I feel my partner is perfect in every other way except these few minor things. If I make them change those things, it will make me so happy.

REFRAMED THOUGHT:

I can suggest those changes, but I understand that it isn't necessary to make me happy. If they choose not to change I'll still be happy with the way they are.

14. FALLACY OF FAIRNESS

CHALLENGE:

• State feelings as a preference rather than an expectation

• Identify what you don't have control over

• Consider other factors and be grateful for what you do have

EXAMPLE THOUGHT:

A friend of mine makes a lot more money at their job doing something similar to me. Why don't I make the same amount, it's not fair they get paid more.

REFRAMED THOUGHT:

I might not make as much money, but I am grateful for the job I have. There could be many reasons why I don't make as much.

15. HEAVEN'S REWARD FALLACY

CHALLENGE:

• Recognize not every sacrifice you make will be rewarded

• State feelings as a preference rather than an expectation

• Separate it from the sacrifice

• Consider other factors

EXAMPLE THOUGHT:

A colleague was promoted over me, but I believe I worked harder and deserved that promotion.

REFRAMED THOUGHT:

It would have been nice to get a promotion, but I can't control other's decisions. I can let my boss know of my hard work, maybe I will be considered next time.

Overcoming Cognitive Distorsions

Challenge thought	Source of distortion	Reframed thought

Overcoming Cognitive Distorsions

Challenge thought	Source of distortion	Reframed thought

Overcoming Cognitive Distorsions

Challenge thought	Source of distortion	Reframed thought

Mindfulness Worksheet

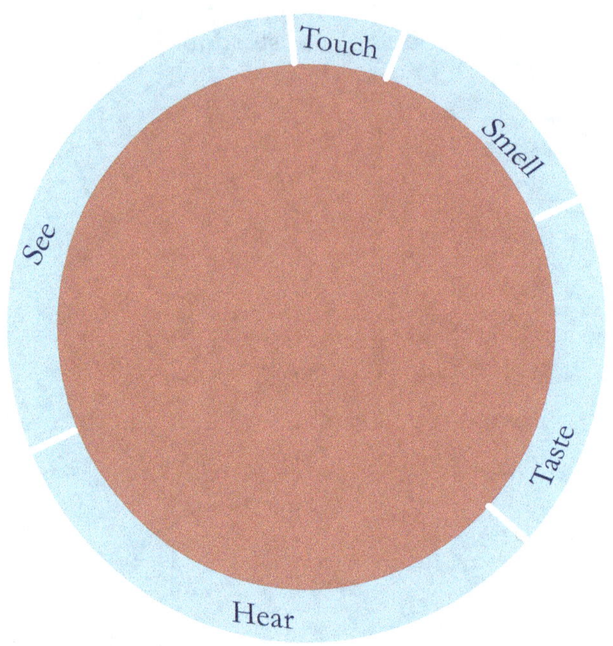

5 Thing you can See

4 Thing you can Hear

3 Thing you can Smell

2 Thing you can Taste

1 Thing you can Touch

Mindfulness Worksheet

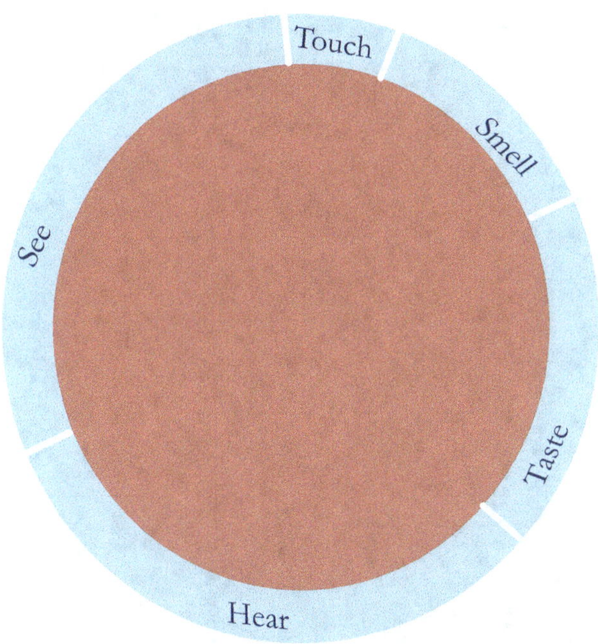

5 Thing you can See

4 Thing you can Hear

3 Thing you can Smell

2 Thing you can Taste

1 Thing you can Touch

Mindfulness Worksheet

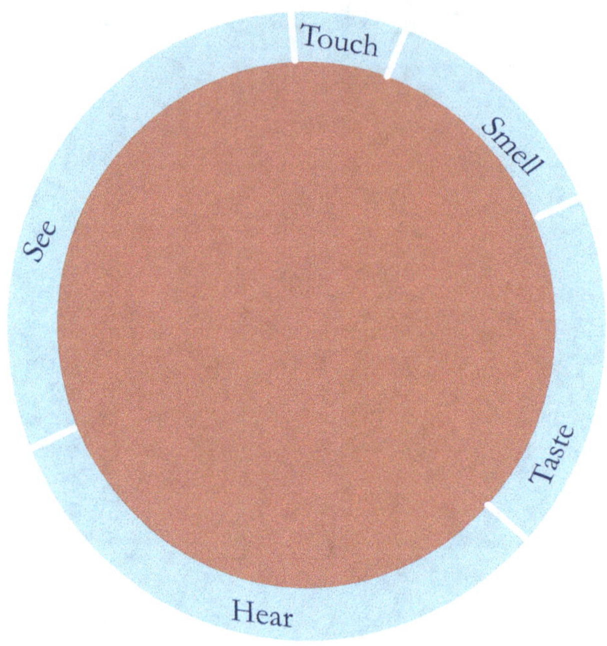

5 Thing you can See	4 Thing you can Hear

3 Thing you can Smell	2 Thing you can Taste

1 Thing you can Touch

Reflection

PART TWO: Thoughts

The most powerful way to manage unwanted intrusive thoughts is to face them deliberately. Each time you calmly and deliberately approach your intrusive thoughts – and you experience that nothing terrible ensues as a result – you train your mind to see them as safe and, eventually, unimportant

The following section puts your thoughts on trial. It's largely our thoughts that lead to moods like depression and anxiety. Thoughts about how things must be, how we should behave, how other people ought to treat us. By changing our thoughts, we can change how we feel.

Thought records are one of many skills taught in CBT. They are based on the premise that you don't have to believe every thought you have. Let's face it, many of our thoughts are half-baked at best and downright wrong at worst.

A thought record is a way of putting your thoughts to the test. It's designed to help you change your moods by finding a more balanced way of thinking about things. In short, you identify a dubious thought and "put it on trial."

The end result of a thought record is a more balanced view. However, in my experience, the process of completing one can be just as beneficial as the end result. When you complete a thought record, you turn your attention inward and notice your thoughts and feelings.

We are often so out of touch with ourselves that we have no idea what we're really thinking or feeling. The process helps you slow down and identify what's going on. When you bring such awareness to your internal experience, there's often a spontaneous shift in how you feel.

Being aware of your thoughts was the first step, but analyzing and reframing your thoughts is what will grow your self-improvement muscle. This section of the workbook should take you 2-3 months to complete

5 step thinking diary

STEP 1: What was I doing (situation/ trigger) ?

Attending a job interview

STEP 2: What are unhelpful feelings/ behaviours (add intensity score 0=low, 10=high)

Feel anxious - 8; feel sick-7; start to perspire - 8

STEP 3: What I was telling myself? (unhelpful negative thoughts/shoulds, oughts, musts)

If i don't get this job it will be awful. The interviewers will see how nervous i am and think i am stupid. I mustn't appear stupid. I shouldn't be here

STEP 4: More helpful or realistic / constructive thoughs I could think instead?

I would like this job- if i don't succeed it does not make me a failure. I can see this interview as a good chance to rehearse. I am calm.

STEP 5: How I might feel or behave in a more helpful/ realistic way?

Relaxed posture - Smile!

Stay calm, keep breathing slowly . Feel in control

NOTES

Actively challenging my unhelpful thinking and using relaxation techniques made me feel more in control

5 step thinking diary

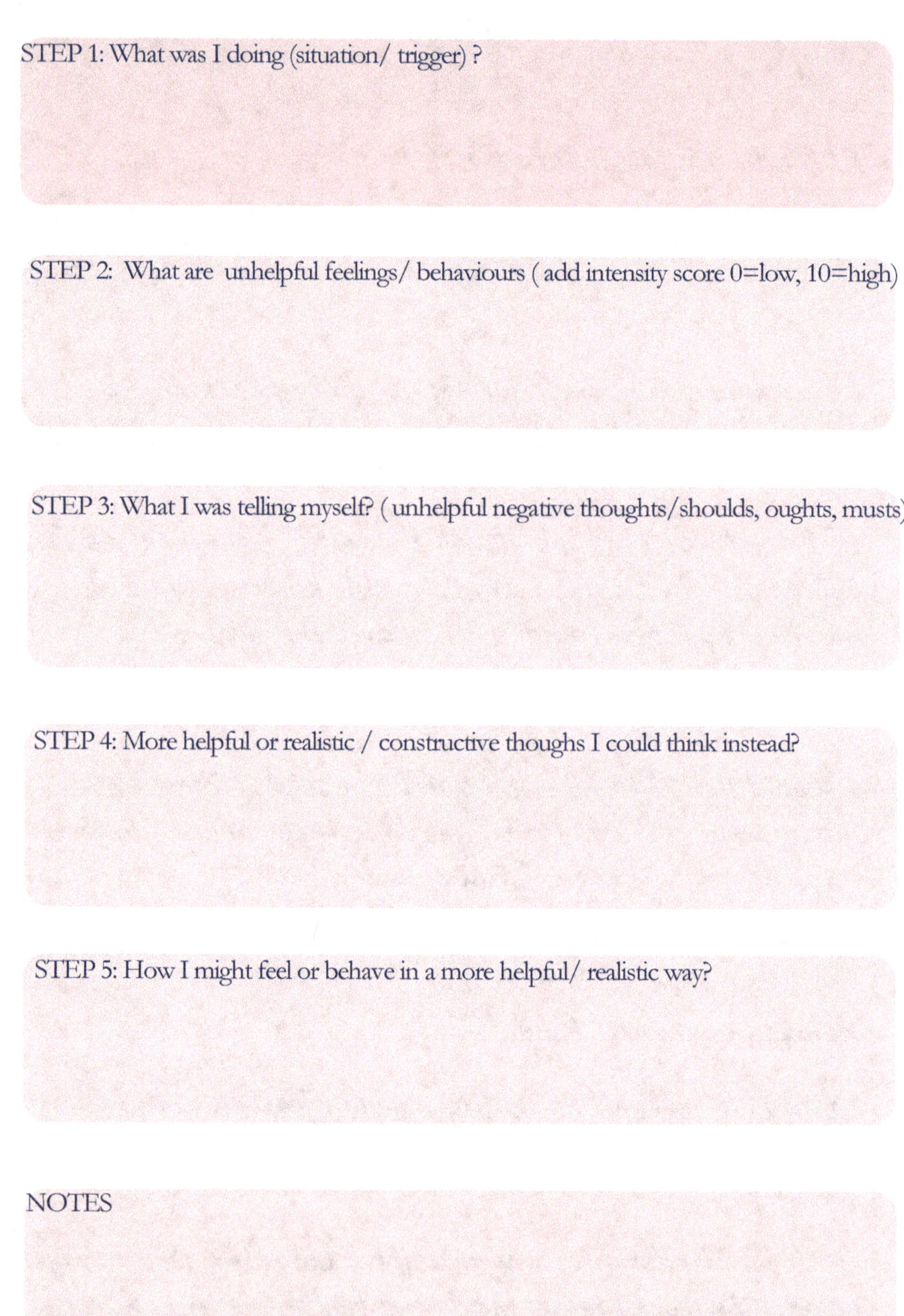

STEP 1: What was I doing (situation/ trigger) ?

STEP 2: What are unhelpful feelings/ behaviours (add intensity score 0=low, 10=high)

STEP 3: What I was telling myself? (unhelpful negative thoughts/shoulds, oughts, musts)

STEP 4: More helpful or realistic / constructive thoughs I could think instead?

STEP 5: How I might feel or behave in a more helpful/ realistic way?

NOTES

5 step thinking diary

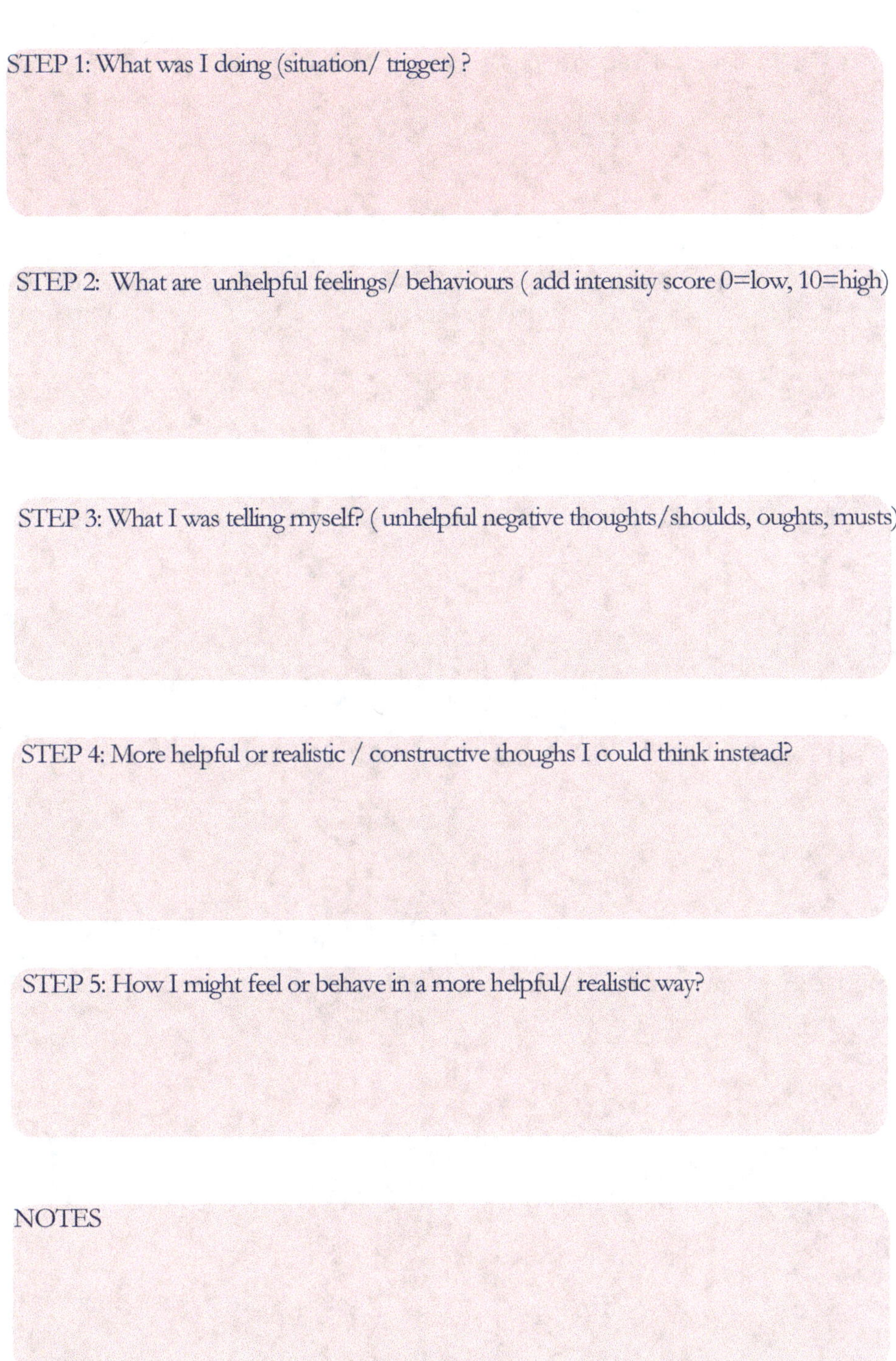

STEP 1: What was I doing (situation/ trigger) ?

STEP 2: What are unhelpful feelings/ behaviours (add intensity score 0=low, 10=high)

STEP 3: What I was telling myself? (unhelpful negative thoughts/shoulds, oughts, musts)

STEP 4: More helpful or realistic / constructive thoughs I could think instead?

STEP 5: How I might feel or behave in a more helpful/ realistic way?

NOTES

5 step thinking diary

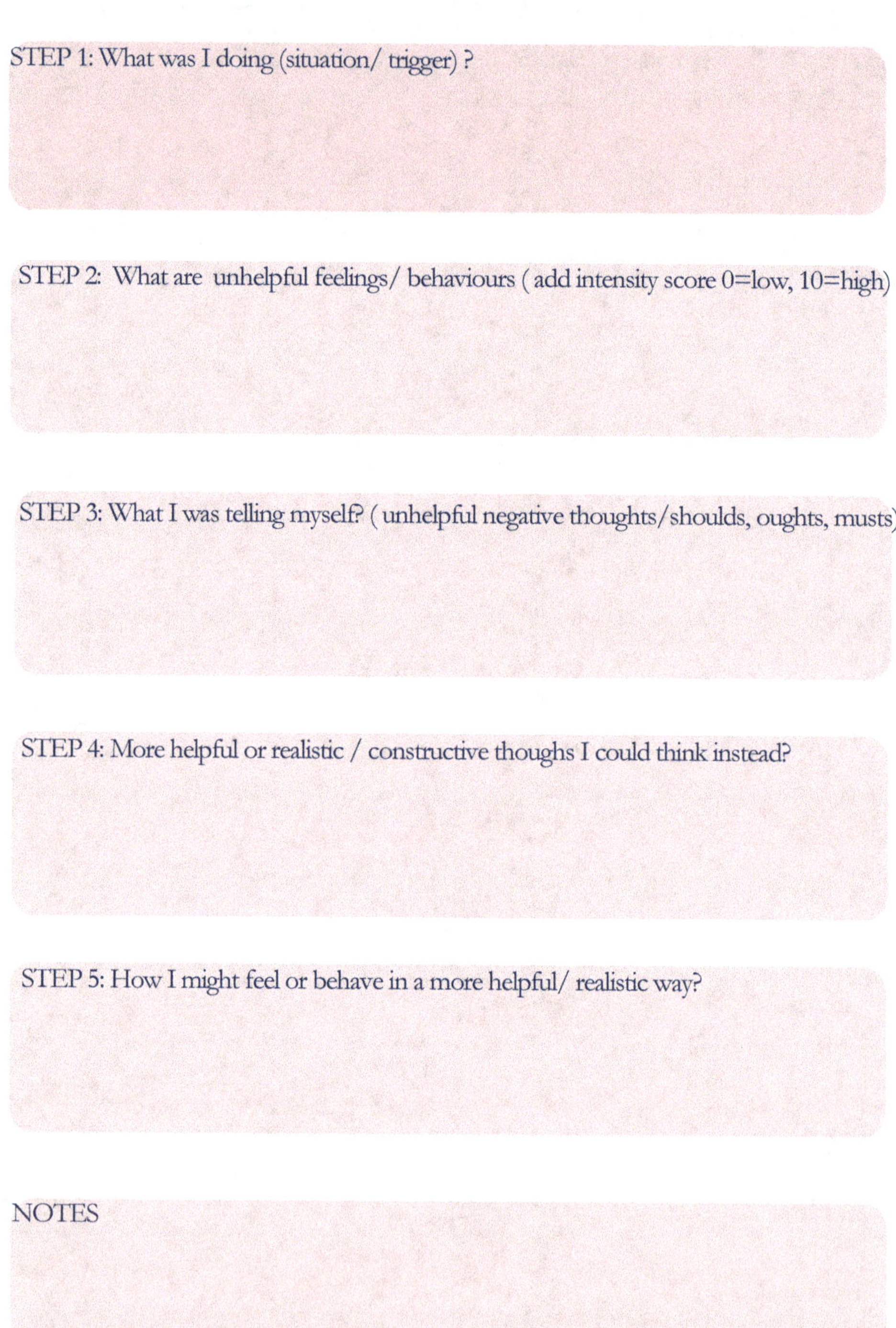

STEP 1: What was I doing (situation/ trigger) ?

STEP 2: What are unhelpful feelings/ behaviours (add intensity score 0=low, 10=high)

STEP 3: What I was telling myself? (unhelpful negative thoughts/shoulds, oughts, musts)

STEP 4: More helpful or realistic / constructive thoughs I could think instead?

STEP 5: How I might feel or behave in a more helpful/ realistic way?

NOTES

5 step thinking diary

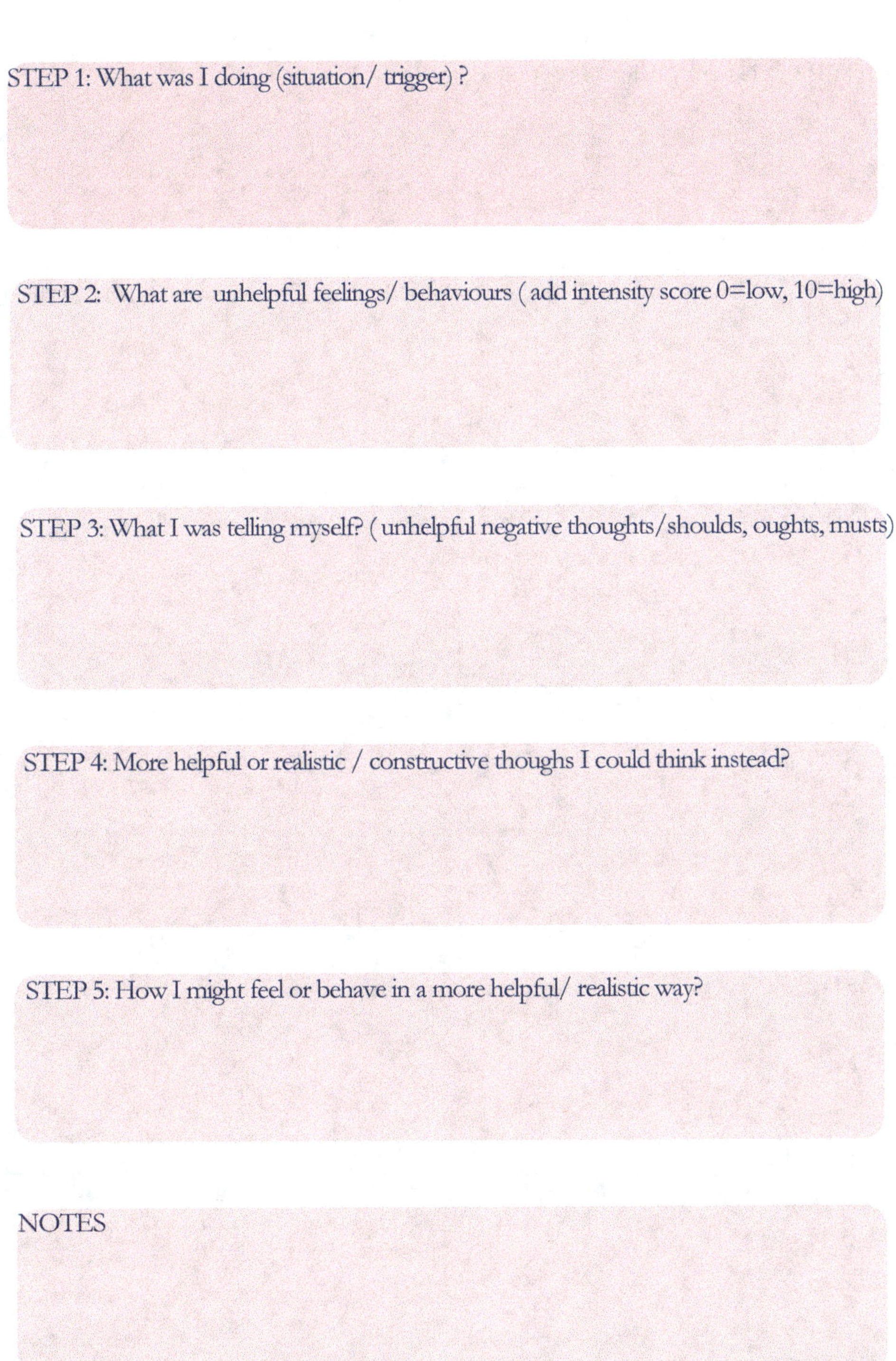

STEP 1: What was I doing (situation/ trigger) ?

STEP 2: What are unhelpful feelings/ behaviours (add intensity score 0=low, 10=high)

STEP 3: What I was telling myself? (unhelpful negative thoughts/shoulds, oughts, musts)

STEP 4: More helpful or realistic / constructive thoughs I could think instead?

STEP 5: How I might feel or behave in a more helpful/ realistic way?

NOTES

5 step thinking diary

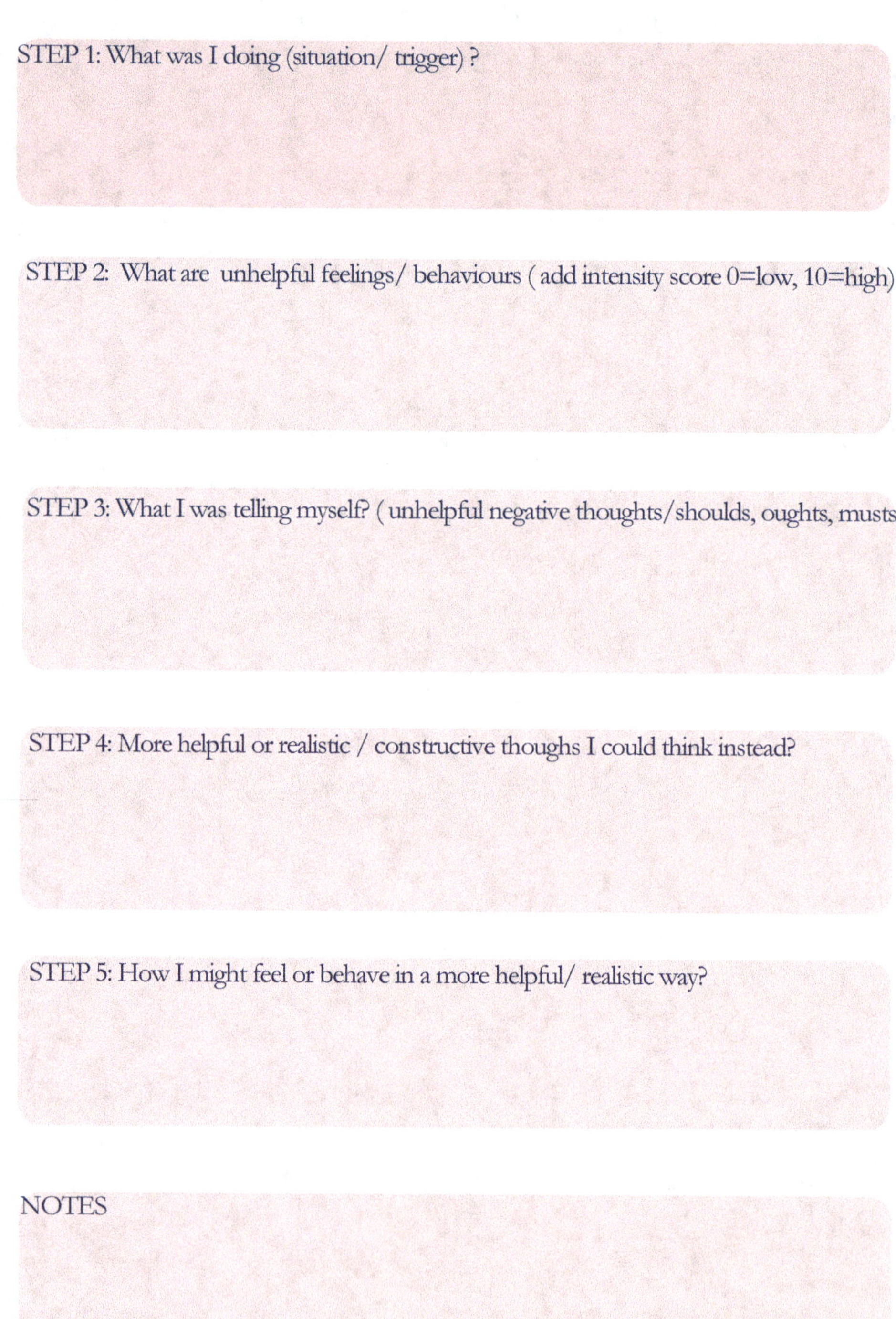

STEP 1: What was I doing (situation/ trigger) ?

STEP 2: What are unhelpful feelings/ behaviours (add intensity score 0=low, 10=high)

STEP 3: What I was telling myself? (unhelpful negative thoughts/shoulds, oughts, musts)

STEP 4: More helpful or realistic / constructive thoughs I could think instead?

STEP 5: How I might feel or behave in a more helpful/ realistic way?

NOTES

Worry Exploration

What are you worried about?

The best that can happen is...

What are some clues that your worry will not come true?

If your worry does not come true how will you handle it?

Worry Exploration

What are you worried about?

The best that can happen is...

What are some clues that your worry will not come true?

If your worry does not come true how will you handle it?

Thought Log

Event	Thoughts or Images	Emotion And Body sensation	Alternate thoughts

Thought Log

Event	Thoughts or Images	Emotion and Body sensation	Alternate thoughts

Challenging Thoughts Worksheet

Negative Thoughts I
Have

Are those thoughts making me
stronger or weaker?

Could my thought be an
exaggeration of what's true?

What would a friend think about this situation?

Is there a better, more empowering way to look at this?

Challenging Thoughts Worksheet

Challenging Thoughts Worksheet

Negative thoughts I have

Are those thoughts making me stronger or weaker?

Could my thought be an exaggeration of what's true?

What would a friend think about this situation?

Is there a better, more empowering way to look at this?

Core beliefs

Core beliefs are opinions or ideas and concepts made by people about themselves and their surroundings throughout a period, after careful observations and ruminations. Whereas automatic thoughts are thoughts that randomly and involuntarily pop into people's minds following a triggering event or situation. But it is important to note that these automatic thoughts are developed or manifested based on the core beliefs possessed by the people.

Core Beliefs

Core beliefs are deeply embedded opinions, and assumptions we possess about ourselves, our surrounding environment and others. These firmly established opinions drastically shape our thoughts, perceptions and our behaviors. It could be said that nothing is more poignant than our core beliefs because they are the root causes of many of our problems, including our automatic negative thoughts.

Core beliefs are just what the name suggests; beliefs. These core beliefs are based on our childhood assessments and are most often inaccurate.

Unfortunately, they are also self-fulfilling. That is, these beliefs only focus on thoughts and facts that support them and reject any idea that goes against those beliefs. Despite all these difficulties it is still possible to overcome their negative impact and change them. The core beliefs are activated when the person is experiencing a stimulating situation. If the situation they are experiencing is negative and threatening in nature their core belief of "I am weak or useless" might get activated. On the other hand, if they are in a less dangerous or threatening situation then their core belief "I am strong or capable" is more likely to be activated. When these core beliefs surface in the person's mind once they get activated they become absolute truths for the person experiencing them.

Core beliefs become harmful when they are not counterbalanced by their alternate versions. As people going through depression strongly experience negative core beliefs and these beliefs are not balanced by their alternative positive counterparts. Thus, these create a harmful environment for the person's mental state.

Automatic thoughts

Automatic thoughts have their roots and foundations in the beliefs that people possess about themselves and the world. But while core beliefs are embedded deep within us while automatic thoughts are surface-level. These are the thoughts that people normally have throughout the day while they live their lives and try to deal with the various life events. In order to identify the automatic thoughts following questions could be asked you recall your automatic thoughts.

- What was going through your mind then?

- What does this mean for you?

- What do other people say about this?

A person experienced plenty of automatic thoughts throughout their time but not all thoughts are as important as others. Some important thoughts help us understand our own thinking process better than the rest of   the thoughts. To help access these thoughts you can record your thinking process to obtain a better understanding of the situation. Just as the name suggests these thoughts pop into our minds directly out of our volition and therefore cannot be controlled by people. A person cannot prevent or eliminate these thoughts as they are reflexive reactions and an outcome of the strongly established core beliefs within us. Fortunately, these thoughts can be challenged and replaced with other thoughts with the help of various techniques such as cognitive restructuring.

Throughout various research studies, it was found that there are a plethora of negative consequences caused due to negative automatic thoughts as opposed to positive automatic thoughts, thus a direct causal relationship between thoughts and consequences.

To help understand it better let us take an example. People suffering from depression and HIV/AIDS at the same time will have negative automatic thoughts associated with depressive symptoms and vice versa. In socially anxious people negative thoughts could deteriorate their anxiety. Also through some research studies, it was found that negative automatic thoughts lead to increased mental health symptoms and reduced levels of self-esteem.

Difference between thoughts and beliefs

While in essence, both are different concepts but since they are so closely interconnected they are often misconstrued as being interchangeable.

Core beliefs are opinions or ideas and concepts made by people about themselves and their surroundings throughout a period, after careful observations and ruminations. Whereas automatic thoughts are thoughts that randomly and involuntarily pop into people's minds following a triggering event or situation. But it is important to note that these automatic thoughts are developed or manifested based on the core beliefs possessed by the people.

As stated earlier beliefs are deeply rooted thoughts, opinions, and observations we believe in firmly due to the countless reaffirmations carried out by us throughout our lives.

A belief could be a very simple thought such as "Everything is hard", or it can be a complicated web of complex thoughts and statements which culminates in the formation of a belief system. We end up affirming the beliefs without consciously being aware of them.

If you listen to yourself you are continually making a case for the 'rightness" of your beliefs even when those beliefs are detrimental to your happiness and well-being! Your "inner lawyer" is continually justifying and being "right" while making other beliefs "wrong". The way to keep a belief system going is to continually affirm it and justify it and never question it.

Our self-concept also plays a major role in the development of negative beliefs and thoughts. Self-concept is the way we perceive ourselves, our experiences, abilities as well as future aspects. It consists of everything that can be used to define us.

Someone who has a negative self-concept is prone to being sensitive about everything and might get affected easily. They could have irrational and negative thoughts such as, " Everybody hates me because I am not likable.

Most importantly, a negative self-concept can lead to an unending cycle of negative thoughts.

Cognitive restructuring

Identifying Distorted Thinking

The first and the most essential step in the process of cognitive restructuring is identifying negative thought processes. The root of all our dysfunctional behaviors and actions is our negative thought process that is developed due to our distorted beliefs. By getting to the root of the problem we can eliminate it. So it is necessary to identify the thoughts that are counterproductive and lead to negative consequences.

Disputing Negative thoughts

By negating the harmful thought processes we can eliminate and thus prevent them from causing further harm.

To dispute the negative thoughts the person needs to ask the following questions to oneself:

- Are my thoughts regarding the event reasonable and valid?

- Is there any evidence or facts that support my view?

- What alternative reasons or perspectives could be for this particular event or situation?

- Am I overanalyzing the situation and drawing unreasonable conclusions?

- What will be the worst-case scenario if my reasoning and thoughts about this   event are correct?

Replacing with Positive Thoughts

The next step is the most crucial. In this step, we replace the negative thoughts that were negated or disputed with positive and enriching thoughts.

These thoughts help bring about a positive change in the person and is beneficial for obtaining adaptive behaviors.

Some things are not within my control and that is fine.

I am allowed to make mistakes

Core Beliefs - example
Examining the Evidence

Core beliefs are a person's most central ideas about themselves, others, and the world. These beliefs act like a lens through which every situation and life experience is seen.

As a person has new experiences, their core beliefs may gradually change. However, some experiences have a greater impact than others. Information that supports a core belief is easily integrated, making the belief stronger. Information that does not support a belief tends to be ignored.

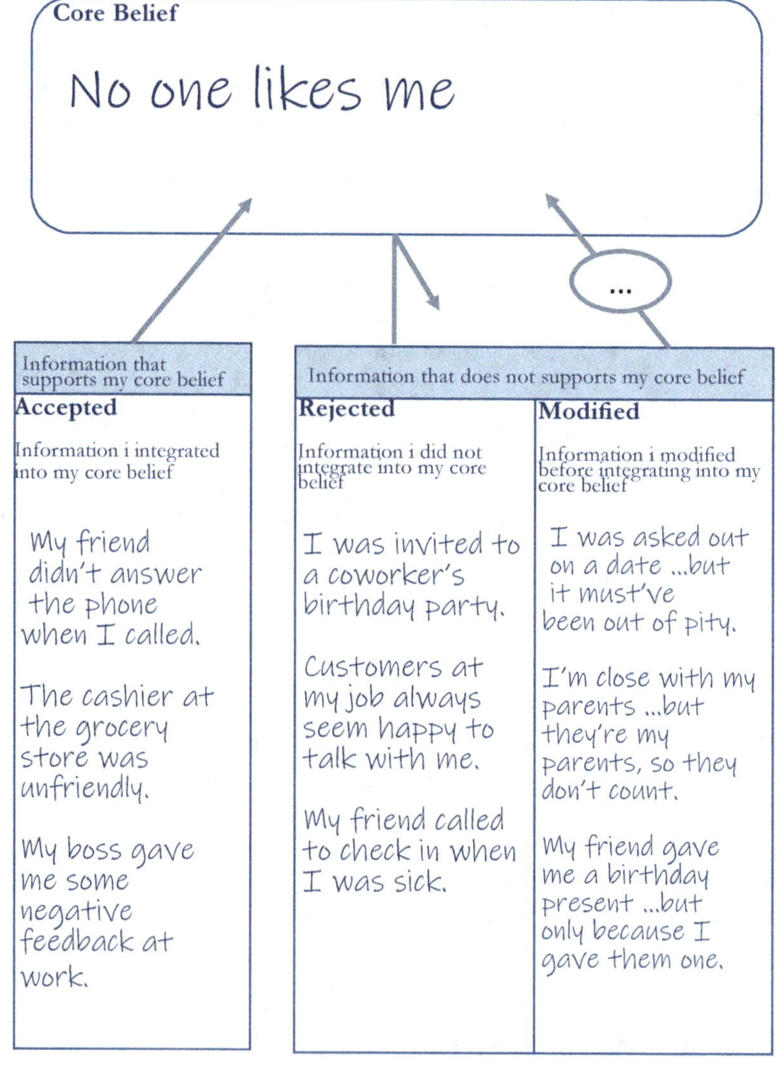

Examining the Evidence

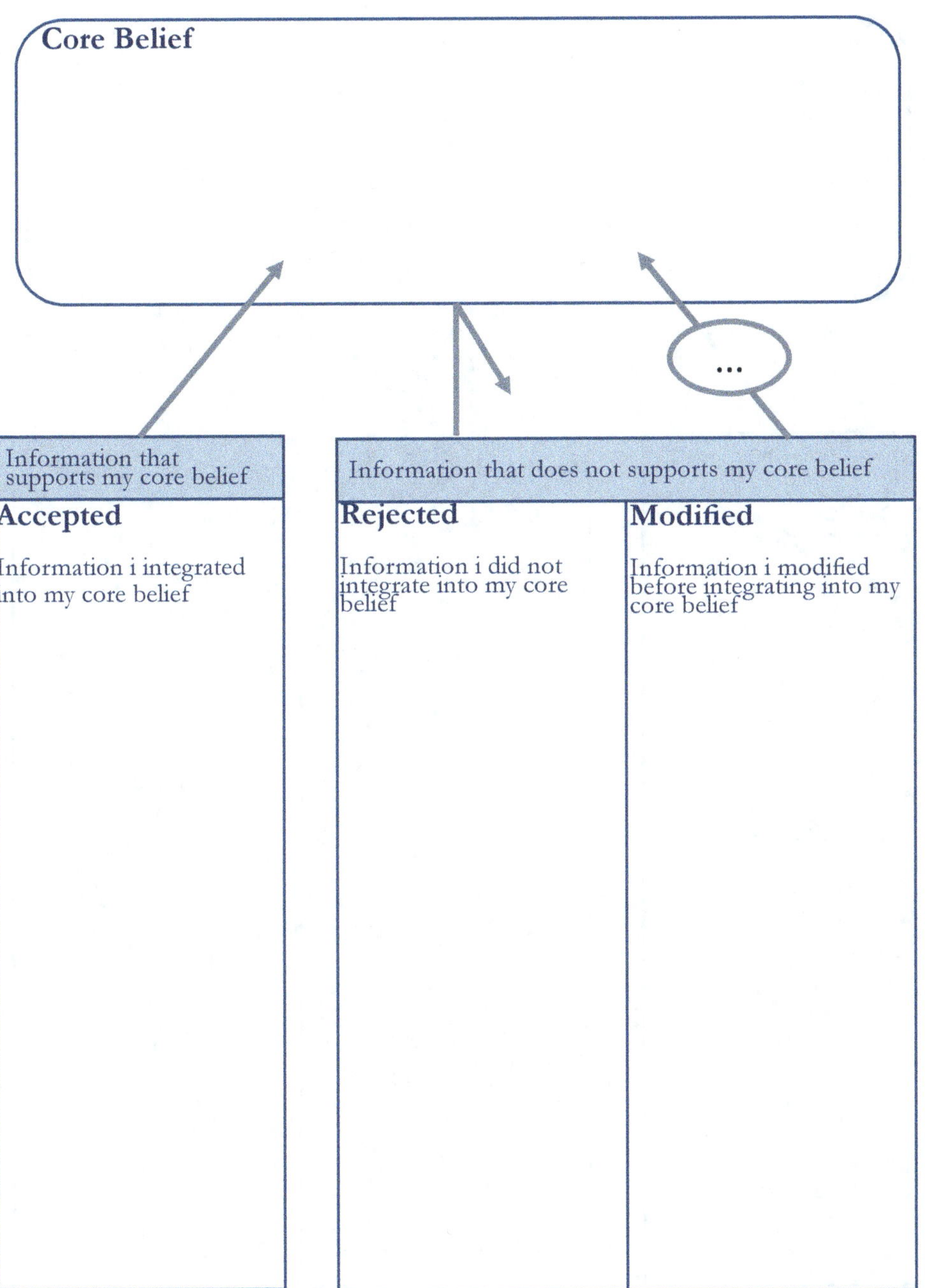

Examining the Evidence

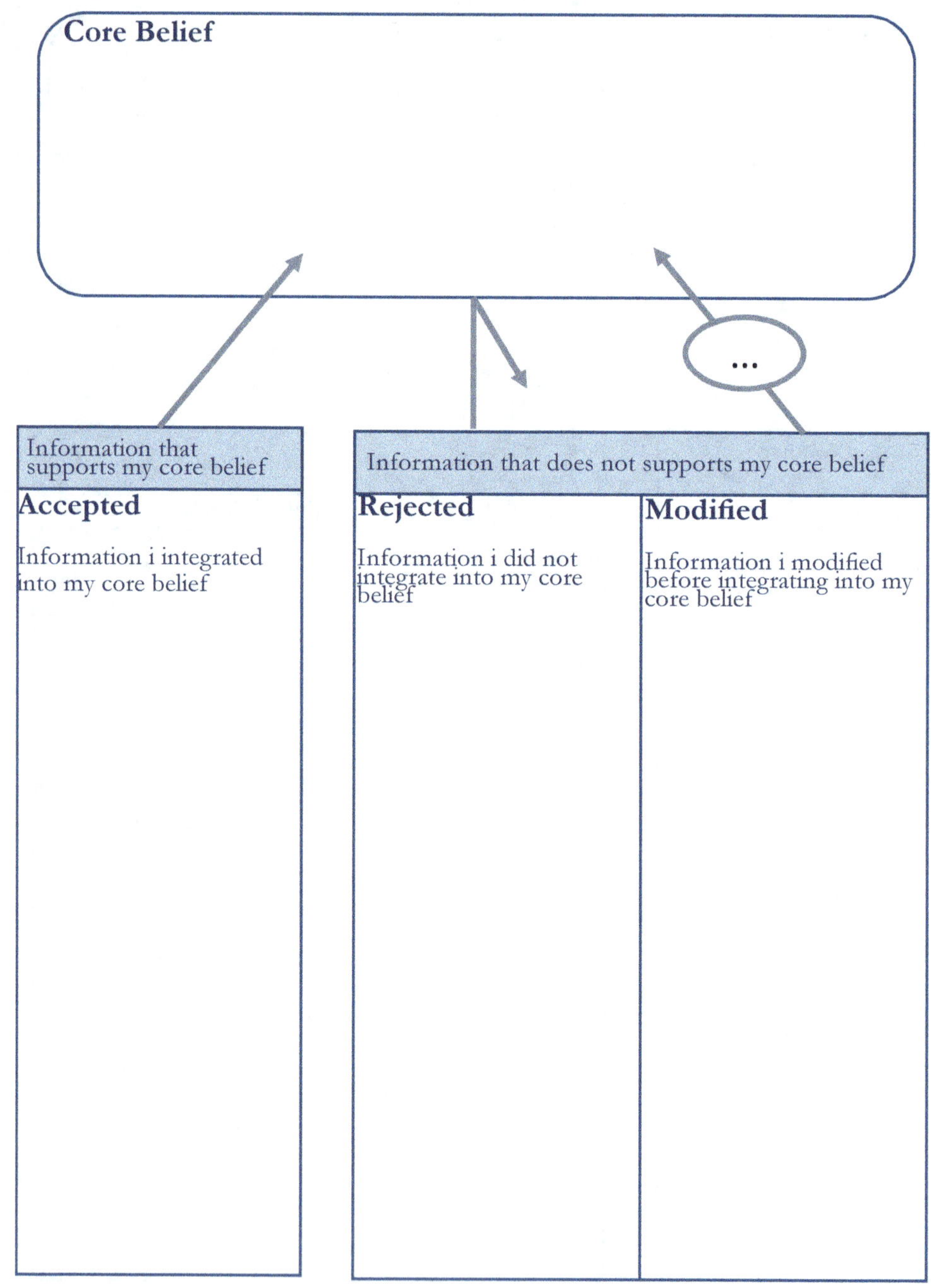

Examining the Evidence

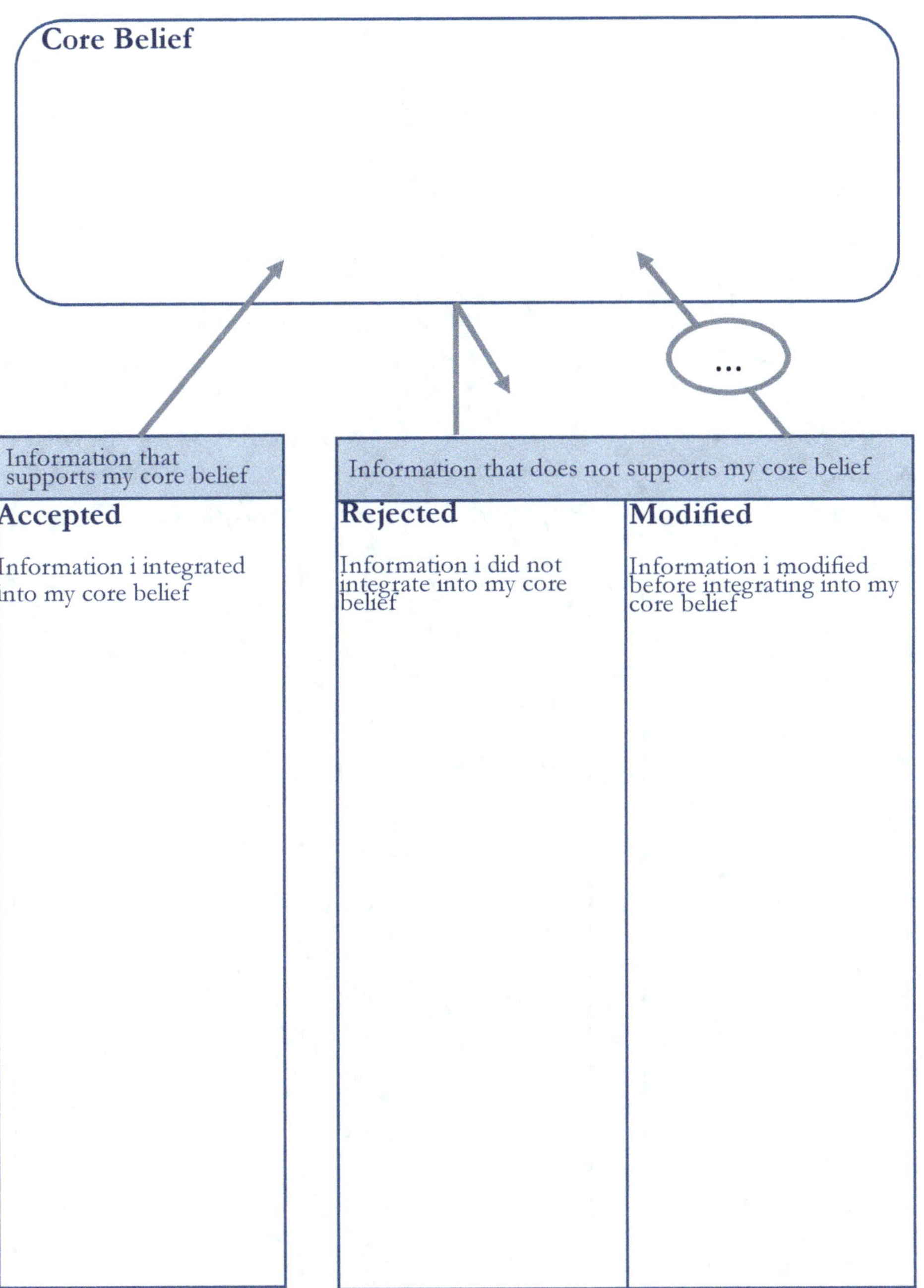

Examining the Evidence

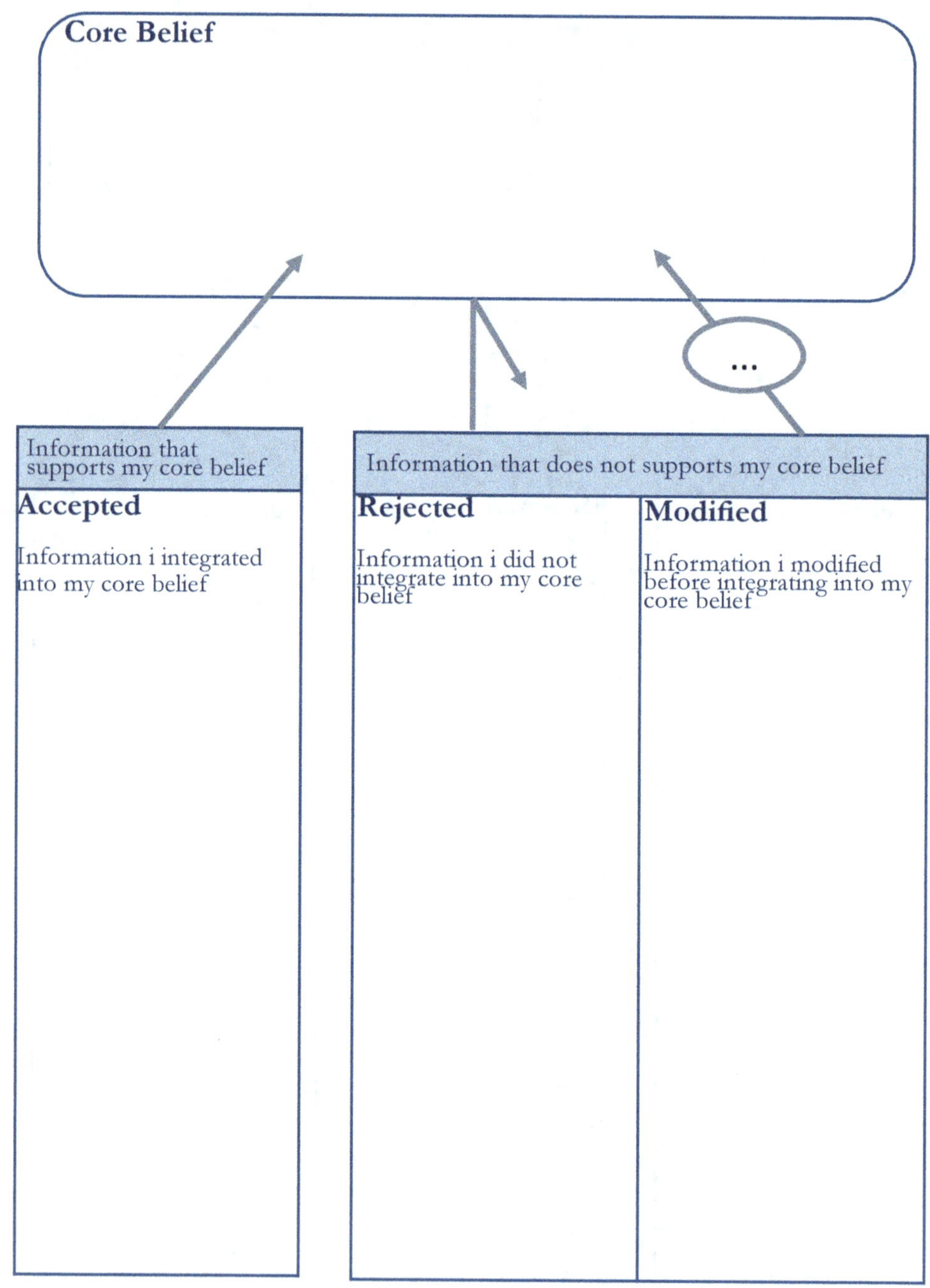

Acceptance Worksheet

Realities that I'm refusing to accept	Ways to accepts the reality

Acceptance Worksheet

Realities that I'm refusing to accept	Ways to accepts the reality

Mood Tracker

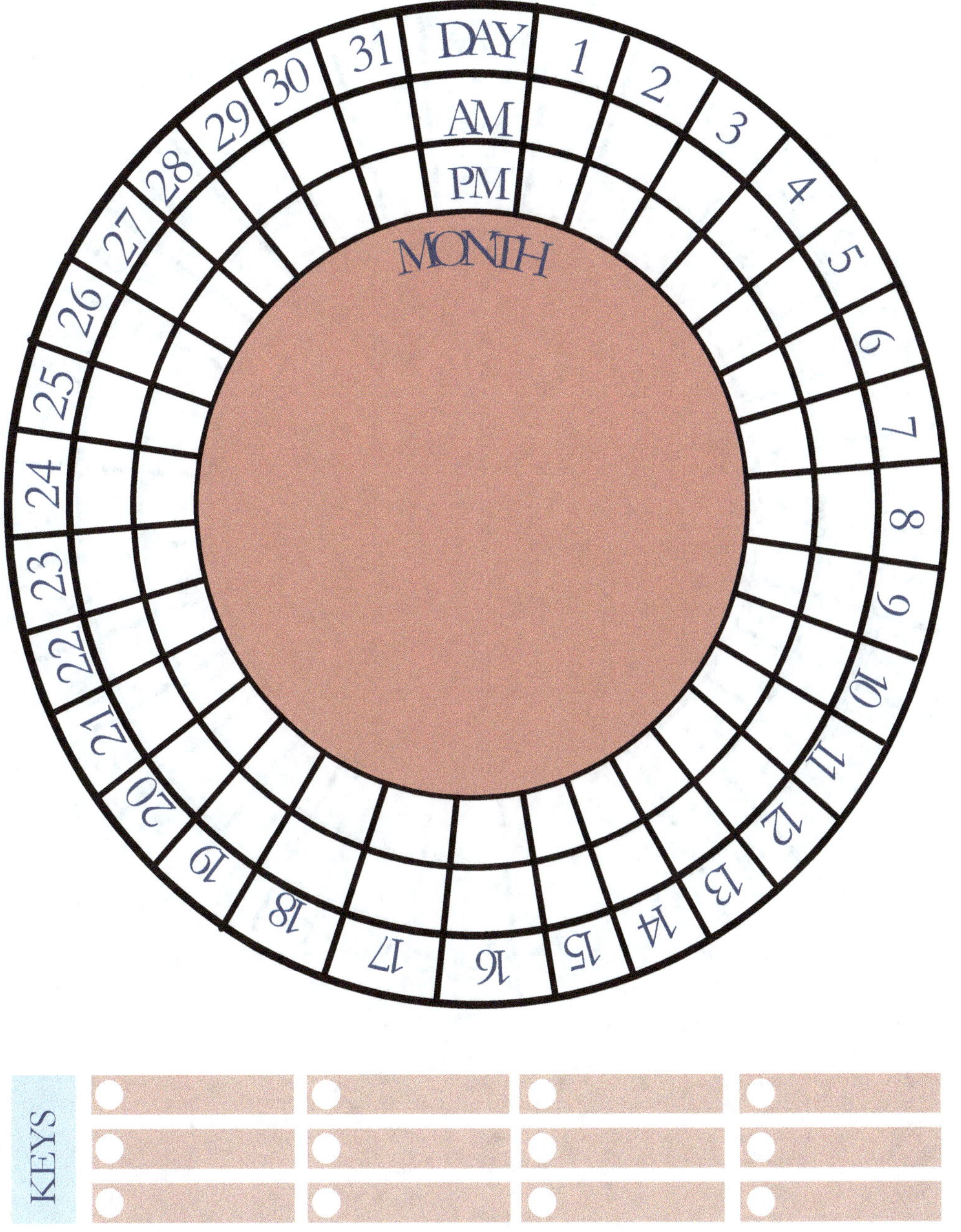

Mood Tracker

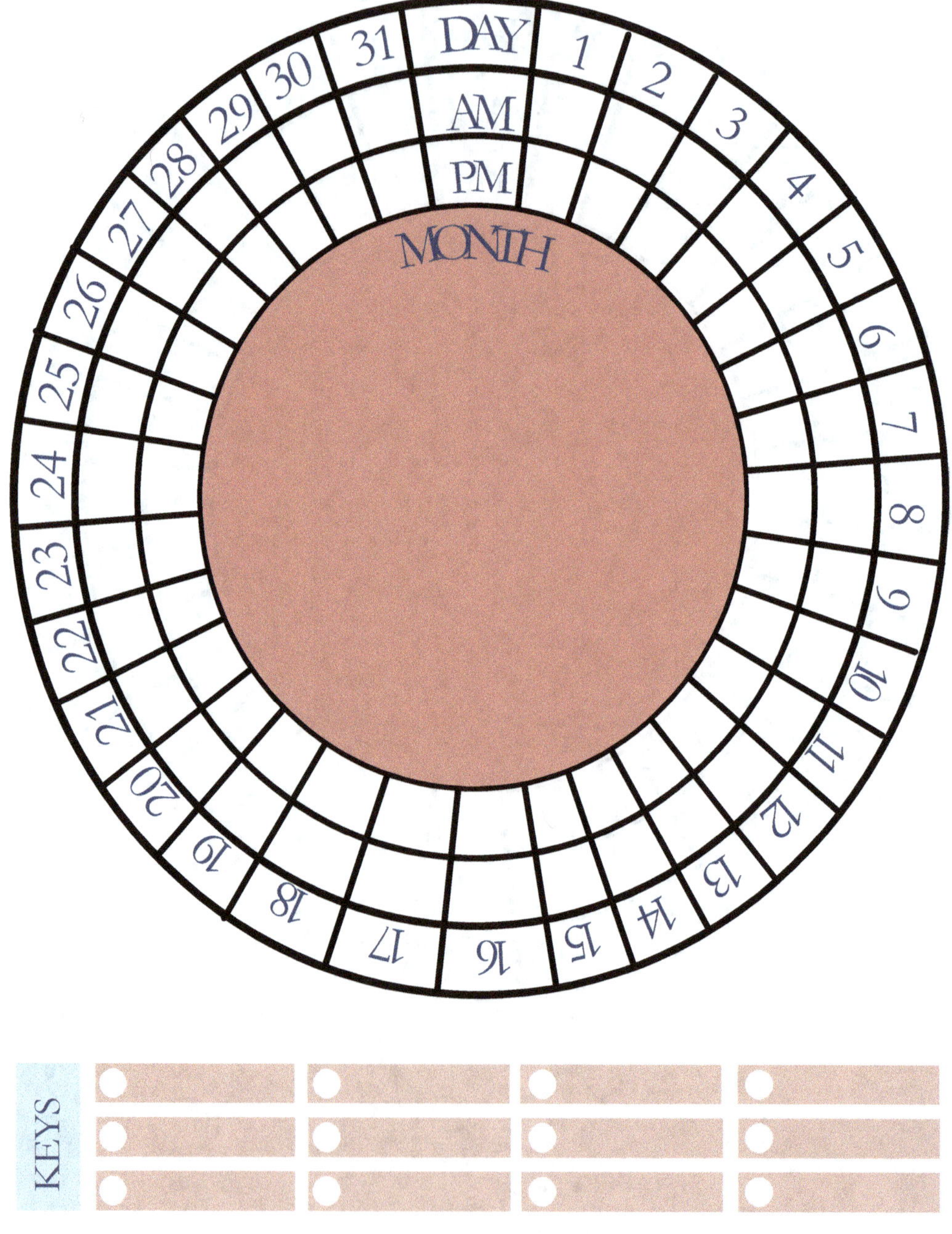

Mood Tracker

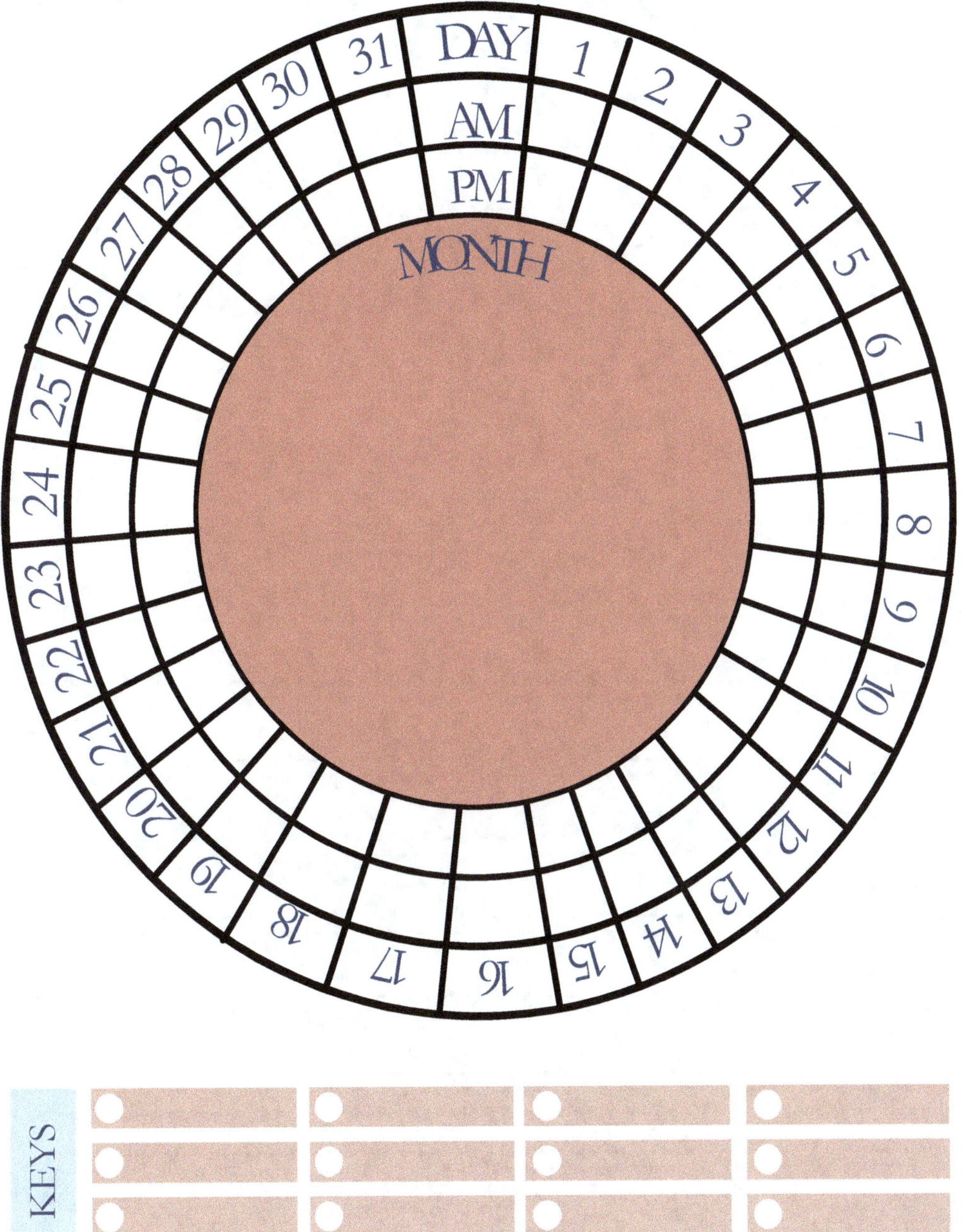

Mindfulness Worksheet

My judgements, interpretations	My feelings, sensation and facts
My judgements, interpretations	My feelings, sensation and facts

Mindfulness Worksheet

My judgements, interpretations	My feelings, sensation and facts
My judgements, interpretations	My feelings, sensation and facts

Managing My Anxiety

Activity	Thoughts And Sensation	Anxiety Level(1-10)

Managing My Anxiety

Activity	Thoughts and sensation	Anxiety level(1-10)

Reflection

PART THREE: Behaviours & Emotions

Now that we have identified and reshaped our negative thinking in a way that changed how we're feeling, now it the time to learn new behaviours and put them into practice.

Activity scheduling and behavior activation If there's an activity you tend to put off or avoid due to fear or anxiety, getting it on your calendar can help. Once the burden of decision is gone, you may be more likely to follow through. Activity scheduling can help establish good habits and provide ample opportunity to put what you've learned into practice.

Behavioral experiments are typically used for anxiety disorders that involve catastrophic thinking. Before embarking on a task that normally makes you anxious, you'll be asked to predict what will happen. Later, you'll talk about whether the prediction came true.

Over time, you may start to see that the predicted catastrophe is actually not very likely to happen. You'll likely start with lower-anxiety tasks and build up from there.

Relaxation and stress reduction techniques. Deep breathing exercises and muscle relaxation help lower stress and increase your sense of control. This can be helpful in dealing with phobias, social anxieties, and other stressors.

Introduction to Emotions

Have you have ever just taken the time to watch the people around you? If you have then you will have contemplated the fact that everyone has a rich inner emotional world. Everyone is at the centre of their own story, with their own heroes and villains, plot twists, struggles and successes. We all want to live happy lives, so why do we find it so hard sometimes?

One popular theory in psychology is that human beings are not evolved to be happy, but instead are 'designed' for survival. If that's true then it changes the rules of the game a bit. Our job becomes one of making sense of how we can inhabit these minds and bodies that are designed for survival instead of happiness, and to live the best lives that we can. In this chapter we're going to learn why emotions are important, and think about some of the ways they can interfere with our lives.

The purpose of emotions

Q: Why do we have emotions?

A: Emotions motivate us, they make us want to do things

Let's do a quick thought experiment. Imagine you woke up one day and didn't have any emotions. How would you decide what to do that day? How would you know what's important and what's not? If you didn't have any emotions would it feel 'nice' to be in a warm, comfortable bed? Would you feel excited about going to work? Or worried about what would happen if you didn't go? What if you had managed to get up and were crossing the road – would you bother to hurry if a car was coming towards you? Why bother to do anything at all?

Our emotions help to guide the decisions that we make every minute of our lives. The world around us (and the thoughts in our heads) trigger emotional reactions all the time. Much of what we do is motivated by a desire to change or maintain a feeling-state – to hold on to good feelings or to avoid bad feelings.

Different emotions motivate us to act in different ways

Have you ever had the urge to shout at someone who was being infuriating? Or the urge to give someone a hug when they were really sad? Have you ever really wanted to take the last piece of cake? All of these urges are driven by our emotions. Emotions make us want to act, and different emotions guide us towards different kinds of actions. The image below shows the variety of actions that our emotions can guide us towards.

Sometimes the actions that our emotions guide us towards can help us to survive, for example:

See rotten food > feel disgust > don't eat the food > don't get sick > survive!

Our emotions are not always a perfect guide to action though. We can choose to listen to what our emotions are telling us but we don't always have to react in the ways they 'want' us to.

 Joy or Happiness can **motivate us** to join in, take part, share.

 Fear can **motivate us** to get away.

 Sadness can **motivate us** to withdraw, brood, ruminate, seek comfort.

 Anger can **motivate us** to attack, lash out, stand up for ourselves.

 Guilt can **motivate us** to repair what we have done.
Shame can **motivate us** to hide away, to keep things secret, to punish ourselves.

 Disgust can **motivate us** to withdraw, keep a distance, get clean.

 Compassion, empathy, or sympathy can **motivate us** to offer comfort, be with.

 Embarrassment or humiliation can **motivate us** to hide.

 Confusion can **motivate us** to check things out (or paralyze us with indecision).

 Powerlessness can **motivate us** to give up.

 Indifference can **motivate us** to ignore.

 Affection can **motivate us** to give love, get close to.

Emotions Motivate Actions

Think about what kind of **action** each of the following emotions might prompt you to take:

Joy or Happiness can **motivate me** to ________________________________

Fear can **motivate me** to ________________________________

Sadness can **motivate me** to ________________________________

Anger can **motivate me** to ________________________________

Shame can **motivate me** to ________________________________

Disgust can **motivate me** to ________________________________

Compassion, empathy, or sympathy can **motivate me** to ________________

Embarrassment or humiliation can **motivate me** to ________________

Confusion can **motivate me** to ________________________________

Powerlessness can **motivate me** to ________________________________

Indifference can **motivate me** to ________________________________

Affection can **motivate me** to ________________________________

Emotions Motivate Actions

Think about what kind of **action** each of the following emotions might prompt you to take:

Joy or Happiness can **motivate me** to ______________________________

Fear can **motivate me** to ______________________________

Sadness can **motivate me** to ______________________________

Anger can **motivate me** to ______________________________

Shame can **motivate me** to ______________________________

Disgust can **motivate me** to ______________________________

Compassion, empathy, or sympathy can **motivate me** to ______________________________

Embarrassment or humiliation can **motivate me** to ______________________________

Confusion can **motivate me** to ______________________________

Powerlessness can **motivate me** to ______________________________

Indifference can **motivate me** to ______________________________

Affection can **motivate me** to ______________________________

How do emotions work in other animals?

In very basic terms, emotions and 'feeling-states' help animals to make decisions about what kinds of things to approach and avoid.

Avoiding things can have huge payoffs. If an animal has an experience of fear when it encounters something new then it will be cautious, or perhaps avoid it entirely. If an animal experiences disgust when it eats a new food it will avoid eating that food in future. These decisions affect the survival of animals: those that are cautious around danger tend to live longer than those that aren't, and bitter-tasting things often contain toxins so it is helpful for animals to have a disgust emotion that says "Hey, don't eat that!". Animals that live longer have more opportunities to reproduce and pass on their genes – and so you (and your genes) are the descendants of ani- mals that did at least some avoiding.

The 'approach' emotions influence survival too. Over millions of years animals have become programmed to enjoy and approach the kinds of things that helped their ancestors stay alive and reproduce. Many different species prefer warmth to cold, being dry to being wet, and prefer eating tasty food. We are animals too – we are the product of millions of years of evolution – and we have much of the same program- ming that makes us want to approach these things that make us feel good.

EMOTIONS THAT MAKE US APPROACH

Why have them?

In our distant past, situations that triggered 'approach' emotions tended to help us fare better. For example if a food tasted good then chances are that it was nutritious and full of energy.

What kinds of things are we programmed to approach?

Food – helps us to stay alive

Sex and intimacy – so that we can reproduce

Comfort (being warm and dry) – helps us to stay healthy

Other people – our ancestors typically survived better in groups than on their own

What problems can happen if this approach system gets out of control?

We might end up doing too much of what we like:

Addictions (over-eating, drug and alcohol problems, compulsive shopping, sex addiction)

Bipolar disorder is a problem where lots of things can feel like a 'good idea' but which can lead us to make unhelpful decisions.

EMOTIONS THAT MAKE US AVOID

Why have them?

In our past, situations that triggered an 'avoid' reaction tended to be ones that threatened our lives or well-being.

What kinds of things can trigger a threat>avoid reaction?

Scary animals

Scary people

Scary situations

The short answer is ANYTHING. Our threat systems are exquisitely sensitive and are designed to learn quickly. If you have ever met someone with a fear or phobia then you have seen the result of an overactive threat system.

What problems are associated with the avoid system being over-active?

Anxiety – a pat of the threat>avoid system

Depression – can be a result of us avoiding things that are essentail for our well-being

Obsessive-compulsive disorder (OCD) – we might try to avoid particular thoughts or consequences

Panic – when we become avoidant of our own body sensations

Emotions as problems

In some ways it is odd to think of emotions as being a problem. After all, it is a normal human experience to feel them, and they are often a good guide to what we need to do. Feeling nervous can make us take care, feeling guilty can guide us to repair any damage we may have caused, and feeling that we have fallen out of love can guide us to end an unhappy relationship. Emotions can cause us to suffer though, so let's think about why this should be the case.

Our evolved emotions and biological 'hardware' may have been programmed to help us survive in the past, but they have to cope with us living modern lives in the 21st century. This makes us vulnerable to a wide variety of problems.

For example, our programming means that we enjoy high-calorie foods. Fat, sugar, and salt typically make us feel good and we seek out more of those foods. This made sense in our evolved environments where energy-rich foods were scarce (when treats are hard to come by it is a good strategy to make the most them while you can). But this desire for salt and sugar-rich food causes problems now that they are readily available. We have to learn to regulate our desires and this isn't always easy.

Another example of our 'programming' concerns other people. Historically, human beings used to live in relatively small groups – you would typically know most of the people in your tribe. 'Outsiders' were often dangerous and it made sense to have a default mode of being suspicious of strangers. The rule doesn't work so well in the modern world. We live in cities with thousands or millions of other people and have no hope of knowing them all. Is it any wonder that some of us are prone to feeling paranoid, suspicious, judged, or anxious?

If you were to take home one message about the evolution of emotions it should really be this: emotions have evolved to help animals to survive, not to make them happy. Given that this is the case, our job becomes one of making sense of how we can inhabit these minds and bodies that are designed for survival instead of happiness, and to live the best lives that we can.

When are emotions a problem?

Some people prefer to view emotions as a guide rather than a problem. When they are feeling something strong they might ask "What is this feeling telling me to do?", or "What does my heart (or gut) tell me?". With the proviso that we are not saying anything is 'wrong' with having emotions, psychologists have some 'rules of thumb' about when emotions can become problematic:

Strong feelings go on for too long

For example, when the (normal) 'baby blues' after giving birth turn into post-natal depression. Or when (normal) strong feelings of grief persist for many years after the loss of a loved one.

They interfere with our ability to live our lives

For example, feeling so anxious that we are scared to leave the house or meet people. Or feeling so sad and demotivated that we can't be bothered to do anything at all. We all have goals (plans) and values (things that are important to us personally) and emotions are worth exploring when they block our progress towards these.

They are out of proportion to what most other people would feel in that situation

For example, a certain amount of shyness is normal but some people feel such para- lyzing anxiety when they are around other people that it is labelled 'social anxiety disorder' (and can be successfully treated). After a traumatic event it is common to feel 'wary' and 'on guard', but some people who develop a condition called post-traumatic stress disorder (PTSD) experience extreme fear that may persist for many years.

We become scared of our own body feelings

Many people become scared of feelings in their own bodies, and in particular what it means to have those body feelings. For example, when Anna was in a place where she felt enclosed she would get short of breath and feel terribly scared. She thought that she must be losing control of her body and worried that she would pass out. Actually she was just noticing normal sensations of anxiety and was in no danger of fainting.

The right amount of emotion

Another way of thinking about the effects of emotion is to sort them into problems of 'too much', 'too little', and 'too difficult to control':

When we feel too much

- We might feel too scared in certain situations, or when confronted with certain things. Sometimes this is labeled anxiety or phobia.
- We might feel scared by what is going on in our own minds, or what we think we might do. Sometimes this is labeled obsessive compulsive disorder (OCD).
- We might worry what other people will think of us, or how they will react. This can be labeled shame or as social anxiety.

When we feel too little

- We might find it difficult to feel pleasure, or we might feel hopeless and lack the motivation to do anything. Depression can be associated with feeling 'numb' or not feeling the right amount of emotion.
- Some people who have experienced significant trauma feel 'numb' or 'detached' from their emotions. This is a common symptom in survivors of trauma who struggle with post-traumatic stress disorder (PTSD).
- Some people who feel emotionally numb can act in quite impulsive ways in an effort to feel something. The lack of emotion can lead to problematic (and sometimes dangerous) ways of behaving.
- Some people who develop psychosis can experience symptoms of 'flat affect' or feel 'emotionally blunted'.

When we can't regulate our emotions effectively

- Some people have moods that cycle between 'highs' where they feel on top of the world (and which often leads to them making irrational decisions) and periods of 'lows' where they experience severe depression. This pattern is often seen in people who suffer from bipolar affective disorder.
- Some people switch very rapidly from feeling quite numb and detached, to feeling strong surges of emotion. This is sometimes called a problem of emotion regulation.
- Some people develop unhealthy ways of managing their emotional states. Examples include people who have developed eating disorders such as anorex- ia or bulimia, or people who self-harm or use substances as ways of managing their emotions.

Exercise:

Managing strong feelings

If you are feeling overwhelmed you could try one (or a few) of the following ways to help yourself

Shift your focus of attention

- Change your environment. Go for a walk, go somewhere new
- Watch a movie, tv show, or a funny video on the internet
- Do something practical. Can you find anything that needs cleaning, painting, or fixing? Do it now
- Read a book

Process your feelings

- Speak to someone about how you are feeling
- Write about how you are feeling (you could write it in a letter to someone, you don't have to post it)
- Draw a picture to represent how you are feeling right now
- Scream into a pillow

Work with your body

- Try a relaxed breathing exercise
- Try a progressive muscle relaxation
- Do some physical exercise. Go for a run, swim, brisk walk, or do some yoga or stretching

Analysis of Problem Behavior

Describe the Situation:

Situation

What are you Thoughts?

Thought

How did you Feel?

Feelings

What were your Behaviors (How did you react?)

Behavior

What was the Outcome?

Outcome

Analysis of Problem Behavior

Describe the Situation:

Situation

What are you Thoughts?

Thought

How did you Feel?

Feelings

What were your Behaviors (How did you react?)

Behavior

What was the Outcome?

Outcome

Analysis of Problem Behavior

Describe the Situation:

Situation

What are you Thoughts?

Thought

How did you Feel?

Feelings

What were your Behaviors (How did you react?)

Behavior

What was the Outcome?

Outcome

Analysis of Problem Behavior

Analysis of Problem Behavior

Describe the Situation:

Situation

What are you Thoughts?

Thought

How did you Feel?

Feelings

What were your Behaviors (How did you react?)

Behavior

What was the Outcome?

Outcome

Fighting Fear

What make you feel nervous or scared	What can be done?
	●
	●
	●
	●
	●
	●
	●
	●

What do you think about when you are nervous or scared

What is something you can do to feel better next time?

Fighting Fear

What make you feel nervous or scared	What can be done?
	●
	●
	●
	●
	●
	●
	●
	●

What do you think about when you are nervous or scared

What is something you can do to feel better next time?

Fighting Fear

What make you feel nervous or scared	What can be done?

What do you think about when you are nervous or scared

What is something you can do to feel better next time?

Fighting Fear

What make you feel nervous or scared	What can be done?

What do you think about when you are nervous or scared

What is something you can do to feel better next time?

Anxiety Worksheet

Date / Time	Situation	Physical sensation	What did I do?	What did I say to myself	Anxiety rating(1-10)
Date / Time	Situation	Physical sensation	What did I do?	What did I say to myself	Anxiety rating(1-10)

Anxiety Worksheet

Date / Time	Situation	Physical sensation	What did I do?	What did I say to myself	Anxiety rating(1-10)

Positive Experiences

Positive Experiences

Courage

Kindness

Selfness

Love

Sacrifice

Wishes

Happiness

Determination

Anxiety Tracker

Date &Time	Trigger What was happening before your began to feel anxiety?	Symptoms Physical, emotional & behavior?	Outcome What helped to calm down?	Anxiety rating

Anxiety Tracker

Date &Time	Trigger What was happening before your began to feel anxiety?	Symptoms Physical, emotional & behavior?	Outcome What helped to calm down?	Anxiety rating

Breathing technique for

anxious moments

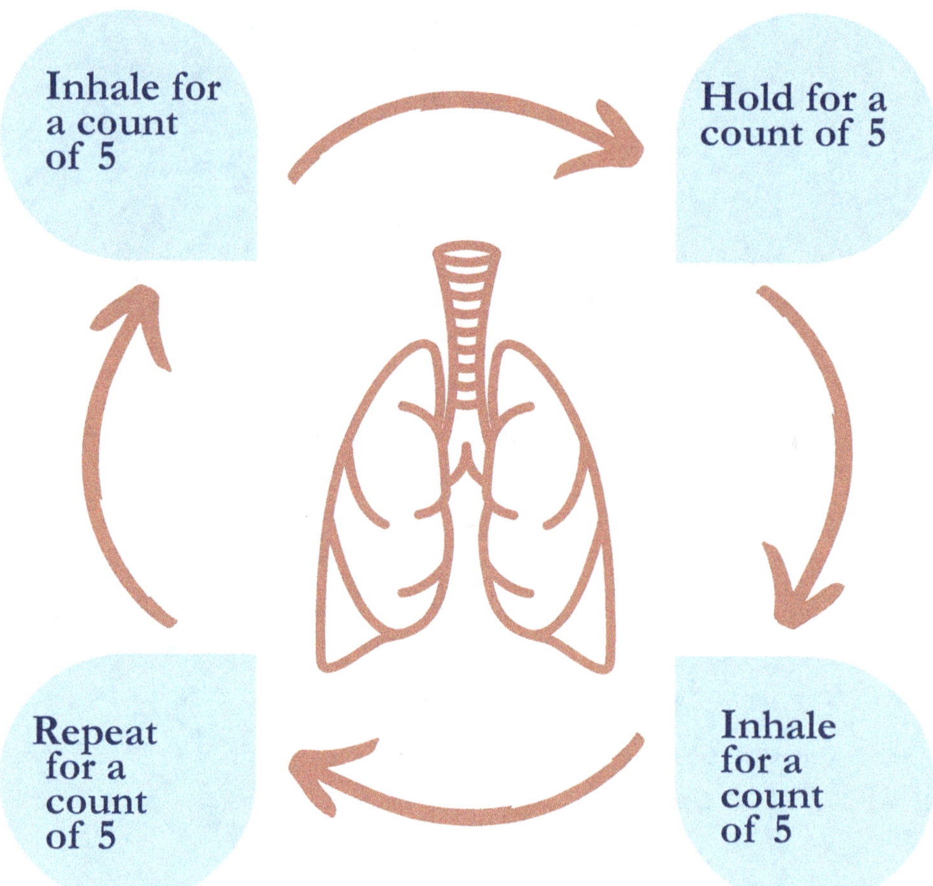

Deep breathing record form

Date and Time	Anxiety level before (0-100%)	Anxiety level after (0-100%)

Deep breathing record form

Date and Time	Anxiety level before (0-100%)	Anxiety level after (0-100%)

Grow Worksheet

How can i reach my goal

My primary goal

Why do i want this?

How will my life be like once I've reached my goal?

Grow Worksheet

How can i reach my goal

My primary goal

Why do i want this?

How will my life be like once I've reached my goal?

Grow Worksheet

How can i reach my goal

My primary goal

Why do i want this?

How will my life be like once I've reached my goal?

Self-Esteem Worksheet

Date:

1	2	3

I felt proud when....

A positive thing I witnessed

Something that made me happy

Self-Esteem Worksheet

Date:

1

2

3

Self-Esteem Worksheet

Date:

1	2	3

Self-Esteem Worksheet

Date: [____________]

My accomplishments this week

1	2	3

I felt proud when....

A positive thing I witnessed

Something that made me happy

Reflection

Reflection

PART FOUR: Action plans

An important first step in overcoming a psychological problem is to learn more about it, otherwise known as "psychoeducation."

Learning about your problem can give you the comfort of knowing that you're not alone and that others have found helpful strategies to overcome it.

You may even find it helpful for family members and friends to learn more about your problem as well. Some people find that just having a better understanding of their problems is a huge step towards recovery.

Depressed or anxious people often attribute positive change to external entities and negative change to themselves. Therefore, at the end of this workbook, is important to recognize your own individual effort and the positive results you achieved (using objective data, such as symptom-rating scales and various trackers available).

By now you have experienced the positive effect of CBT:

- Identifying your thought patterns.

- Discovering how your thoughts affect your feelings and behaviors.

- Determining if your thoughts are accurate.

- Replacing biased thoughts with more realistic ones.

- That scheduling activities will bring you enjoyment and a sense of success

- Recognizing how your actions influence your thoughts and emotions.

- Making the best use of your time.

- Breaking down daunting tasks into more manageable ones.

- Facing your fears gradually so they diminish

This section will take you 3 months to complete.

Keep practicing your CBT skills! This is the best way to prevent a relapse. If you're practicing regularly, you'll be in good shape to handle whatever situations you're faced with.

Next Goal Setting

Goal	Motivation

Start Date:

Due Date:

Possible obstacles

Milestone

How to overcome these obstacles

Action Steps

My Main Goals

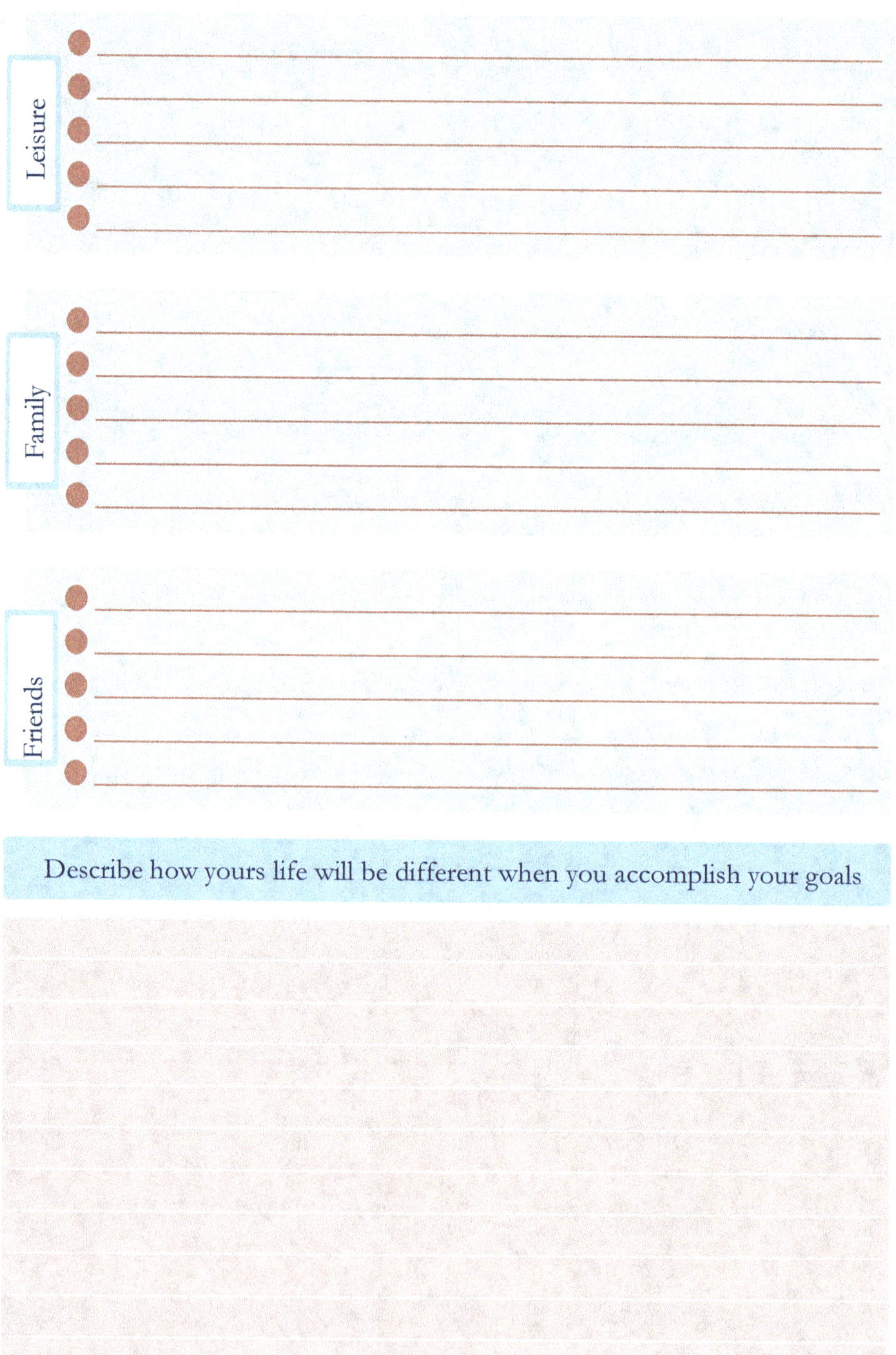

Describe how yours life will be different when you accomplish your goals

My Main Goals

Finances	Volunteering Or Contributions	Physical Health

Education	Mental Health	Work Or Project

Home Environment

Next Goal Setting

Goal	Motivation

Start Date:

Due Date:

Possible obstacles	Milestone

How to overcome these obstacles

Action steps

Monthly Planner

Month:

Sunday					
Monday					
Tuesday					
Wednesday					
Thursday					
Friday					
Saturday					

Monthly Reflection

How i feel about this month?

- ____________________
- ____________________
- ____________________
- ____________________
- ____________________
- ____________________
- ____________________
- ____________________
- ____________________
- ____________________
- ____________________
- ____________________
- ____________________

What changed since last month?

- ____________________
- ____________________
- ____________________
- ____________________
- ____________________
- ____________________
- ____________________
- ____________________
- ____________________
- ____________________
- ____________________
- ____________________
- ____________________

My accomplishments this month

- ____________________
- ____________________
- ____________________
- ____________________
- ____________________
- ____________________
- ____________________
- ____________________
- ____________________
- ____________________
- ____________________
- ____________________

What i want to improve next month?

- ____________________
- ____________________
- ____________________
- ____________________
- ____________________
- ____________________
- ____________________
- ____________________
- ____________________
- ____________________
- ____________________
- ____________________

Monthly Planner

Month:

<table>
<tr><td>Sunday</td><td></td><td></td><td></td><td></td><td></td></tr>
<tr><td>Monday</td><td></td><td></td><td></td><td></td><td></td></tr>
<tr><td>Tuesday</td><td></td><td></td><td></td><td></td><td></td></tr>
<tr><td>Wednesday</td><td></td><td></td><td></td><td></td><td></td></tr>
<tr><td>Thursday</td><td></td><td></td><td></td><td></td><td></td></tr>
<tr><td>Friday</td><td></td><td></td><td></td><td></td><td></td></tr>
<tr><td>Saturday</td><td></td><td></td><td></td><td></td><td></td></tr>
</table>

Monthly Reflection

Monthly Planner

Month:

Sunday

Monday

Tuesday

Wednesday

Thursday

Friday

Saturday

Monthly Reflection

How i feel about this month?

What changed since last month?

My accomplishments this month

What i want to improve next month?

Reflection

PART FIVE: Preventing relapse

Managing your problem effectively is a lot like exercise – you need to "keep in shape" and make practicing the helpful skills a daily habit. However, sometimes people slip back into old habits, lose the improvements they've made and have a relapse. A relapse is a complete return to all of your old ways of thinking and behaving before you learned new strategies for managing your problem. While it's normal for people to experience lapses (a brief return to old habits) during times of stress, low mood or fatigue, a relapse certainly does not have to take place. Here are some tips on how to prevent lapses and relapses:

Know when you are more vulnerable to having a lapse (e.g., during times of stress or change), and you'll be less likely to have one. It also helps to make a list of warning signs (e.g., more anxious thoughts, frequent arguments with loved ones) that tell you your anxiety might be increasing. Once you know what your warning signs or "red flags" are, you can then make an action plan to cope with them. This might involve, for example, practicing some CBT skills like calm breathing or challenging your negative thinking.

Remember that, like everyone else on earth, you are a work in progress! A good way to prevent future lapses is to continue working on new challenges. You're less likely to slide back into old habits if you're continually working on new and different ways of overcoming your anxiety.

If you have had a lapse, try to figure out what situation led you to it. This can help you make a plan to cope with difficult situations in the future. Keep in mind that it's normal to occasionally have lapses and that you can learn a lot from them.

PART FIVE: Preventing relapse

If you have had a lapse, try to figure out what situation led you to it. This can help you make a plan to cope with difficult situations in the future. Keep in mind that it's normal to occasionally have lapses and that you can learn a lot from them.

How you think about your lapse has a huge impact on your later behaviour. If you think that you're a failure and have undone all your hard work, you're more likely to stop trying and end up relapsing. Instead, it's important to keep in mind that it's impossible to unlearn all the skills and go back to square one (i.e., having anxiety and not knowing how to handle it) because you do know how to handle your anxiety. If you have a lapse, you can get back on track. It's like riding a bike: once you know how to ride one, you don't forget it! You might become a bit rusty, but it won't be long until you're as good as before.

Remember that lapses are normal and can be overcome. Don't beat yourself up or call yourself names like "idiot" or "loser," because this doesn't help. Be kind to yourself, and realize that we all make mistakes sometimes!

Finally, make sure to reward yourself for all the hard work you're doing. A reward might be going out for a nice meal or buying yourself a little treat. Managing anxiety or depression is not always easy or fun, and you deserve a reward for your hard work!

If you have had a lapse, try to figure out what situation led you to it. This can help you make a plan to cope with difficult situations in the future. Keep in mind that it's normal to occasionally have lapses and that you can learn a lot from them.

My safety plan

My warning signs are:

My effective copying strategies are:

People I can reach out to for distraction:

Person 1:

Person 2:

Person 3:

People I can reach out to for help

Person 1:

Person 2:

Person 3:

Step I can take to make my environment beter:

In the event of the crisis:

Problem solving worksheet

| Problem to solve | End soal |

| 1st solution | Pros | Cons |

| 2nd solution | Pros | Cons |

| 3rd solution | Pros | Cons |

| Choosen solution | Next step |

Problem solving worksheet

Problem to solve	End goal

1st solution	Pros	Cons

2nd solution	Pros	Cons

3rd solution	Pros	Cons

Choosen solution	Next step

A reminder to myself

I like the fact that i...

I feel great when...

My skills are strengths are...

i love being myself when....

A reminder to myself

I like the fact that i...

I feel great when...

My skills are strengths are...

i love being myself when....

Letter of Forgivness

I Forgive Myself	Next Time I Will

I Forgive Myself	Next Time I Will

Letter of Forgivness

I Forgive Myself	Next Time I Will

Positive Affirmation List

1.
2.
3.
4.
5.
6.
7.
8.
9.
10.
11.
12.
13.
14.
15.
16.
17.
18.
19.
20.

Positive Affirmation List

1
2
3
4
5
6
7
8
9
10
11
12
13
14
15
16
17
18
19
20

Reflection

PART SIX: Suporting materials

In the next pages you have some suporting materials not specifically discussed in the previous chapters. These might be relevant when you want to track your progress on specific elements. (sleep, symptoms, medication, food and water intake, etc.)

That's it for now! We would love to hear from you. Your opinion matters. Comment with your feedback on the purchase platform and rate this workbook if you find it useful. Please provide us with your ideas of what could be improved or if you are missing something from this book.

We look forward to hear your success stories and how this CBT workbook has helped you - it will create a positive change and inspire others.

If you are looking for a CBT therapist or coach, reach out to the author of this workbook on www.cproject.nl or check-out thousands of other mental professionals on www.betterhelp.com

Alternately, if you're looking for specific tools or more advanced CBT techniques, feel free to check the resources available at www.psychologytools.com; www.therapistaid.com or www.cbtpsychology.com

Sensation Record

Activity	Thoughts And Sensation	Anxiety Level(1-10)

Sensation Record

Activity	Thoughts And Sensation	Anxiety Level(1-10)

Exercise Tracker

Exercise

M T W T F S S

Exercise Tracker

Exercise

	M	T	W	T	F	S	S

Food Tracker

DAY	TIME	MEAL/SNACK/BEVERAGE	QUANTITY	COMMENTS

Food Tracker

DAY	TIME	MEAL/SNACK/BEVERAGE	QUANTITY	COMMENTS

Self-Care Tracker

Month: ________

Self Care Action

	M	T	W	T	F	S	S
	☐	☐	☐	☐	☐	☐	☐
	☐	☐	☐	☐	☐	☐	☐
	☐	☐	☐	☐	☐	☐	☐
	☐	☐	☐	☐	☐	☐	☐
	☐	☐	☐	☐	☐	☐	☐
	☐	☐	☐	☐	☐	☐	☐
	☐	☐	☐	☐	☐	☐	☐
	☐	☐	☐	☐	☐	☐	☐
	☐	☐	☐	☐	☐	☐	☐
	☐	☐	☐	☐	☐	☐	☐
	☐	☐	☐	☐	☐	☐	☐
	☐	☐	☐	☐	☐	☐	☐
	☐	☐	☐	☐	☐	☐	☐
	☐	☐	☐	☐	☐	☐	☐
	☐	☐	☐	☐	☐	☐	☐

Self-Care Tracker

Month:

Self Care Action

	M	T	W	T	F	S	S
	☐	☐	☐	☐	☐	☐	☐
	☐	☐	☐	☐	☐	☐	☐
	☐	☐	☐	☐	☐	☐	☐
	☐	☐	☐	☐	☐	☐	☐
	☐	☐	☐	☐	☐	☐	☐
	☐	☐	☐	☐	☐	☐	☐
	☐	☐	☐	☐	☐	☐	☐
	☐	☐	☐	☐	☐	☐	☐
	☐	☐	☐	☐	☐	☐	☐
	☐	☐	☐	☐	☐	☐	☐
	☐	☐	☐	☐	☐	☐	☐
	☐	☐	☐	☐	☐	☐	☐
	☐	☐	☐	☐	☐	☐	☐
	☐	☐	☐	☐	☐	☐	☐
	☐	☐	☐	☐	☐	☐	☐

Symptoms Tracker

Rate From 1-10 How Was Your Week And Put The Number Into The Rectangle

Mental Symptoms

	M	T	W	T	F	S	S
	☐	☐	☐	☐	☐	☐	☐
	☐	☐	☐	☐	☐	☐	☐
	☐	☐	☐	☐	☐	☐	☐
	☐	☐	☐	☐	☐	☐	☐
	☐	☐	☐	☐	☐	☐	☐
	☐	☐	☐	☐	☐	☐	☐
	☐	☐	☐	☐	☐	☐	☐
	☐	☐	☐	☐	☐	☐	☐
	☐	☐	☐	☐	☐	☐	☐
	☐	☐	☐	☐	☐	☐	☐

Physical Symptoms

	M	T	W	T	F	S	S
	☐	☐	☐	☐	☐	☐	☐
	☐	☐	☐	☐	☐	☐	☐
	☐	☐	☐	☐	☐	☐	☐
	☐	☐	☐	☐	☐	☐	☐
	☐	☐	☐	☐	☐	☐	☐
	☐	☐	☐	☐	☐	☐	☐
	☐	☐	☐	☐	☐	☐	☐
	☐	☐	☐	☐	☐	☐	☐
	☐	☐	☐	☐	☐	☐	☐
	☐	☐	☐	☐	☐	☐	☐

Symptoms Tracker

Rate From 1-10 How Was Your Week And Put The Number Into The Rectangle

Mental Symptoms

	M	T	W	T	F	S	S

Physical Symptoms

	M	T	W	T	F	S	S

Period Tracker

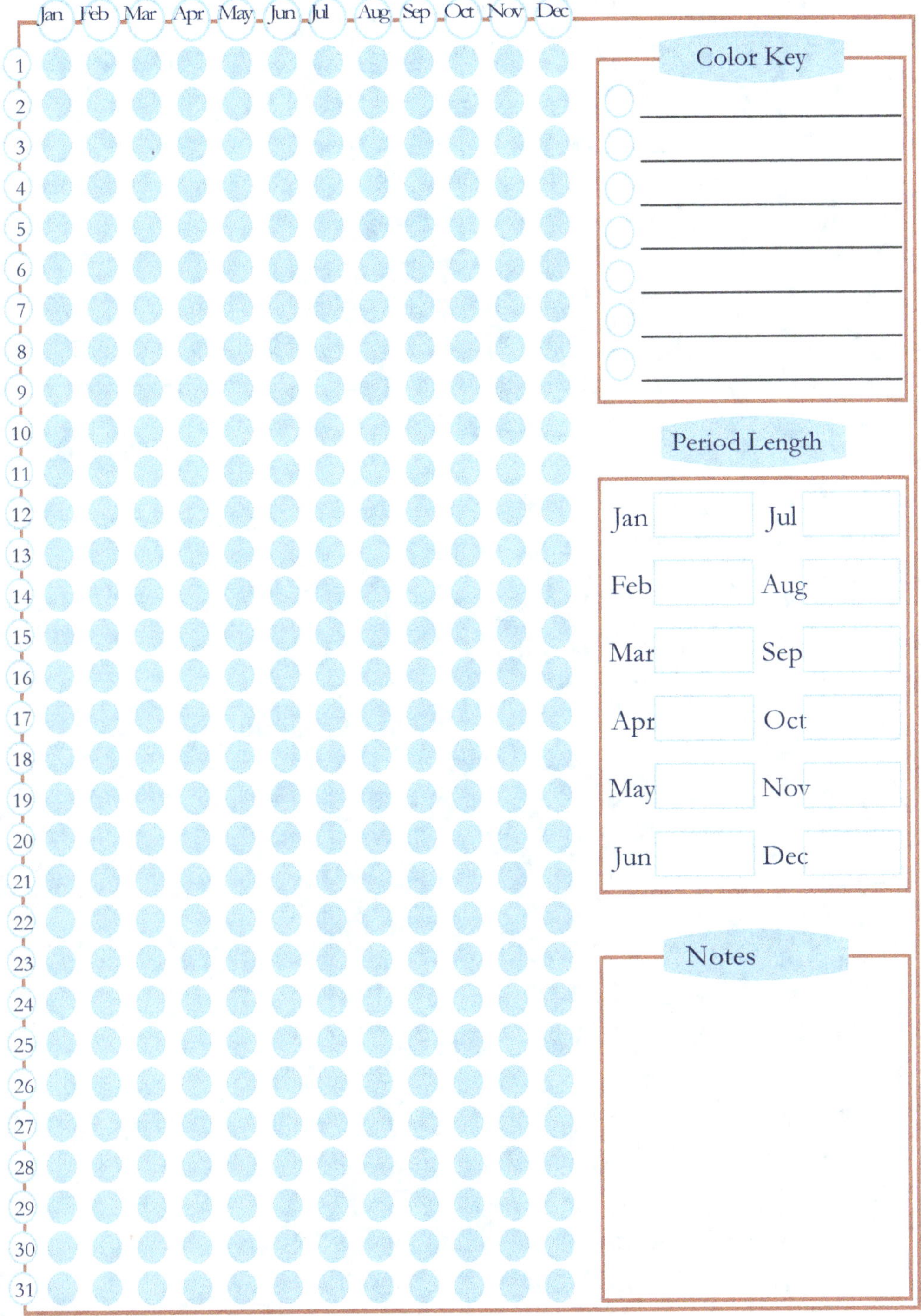

Period Tracker

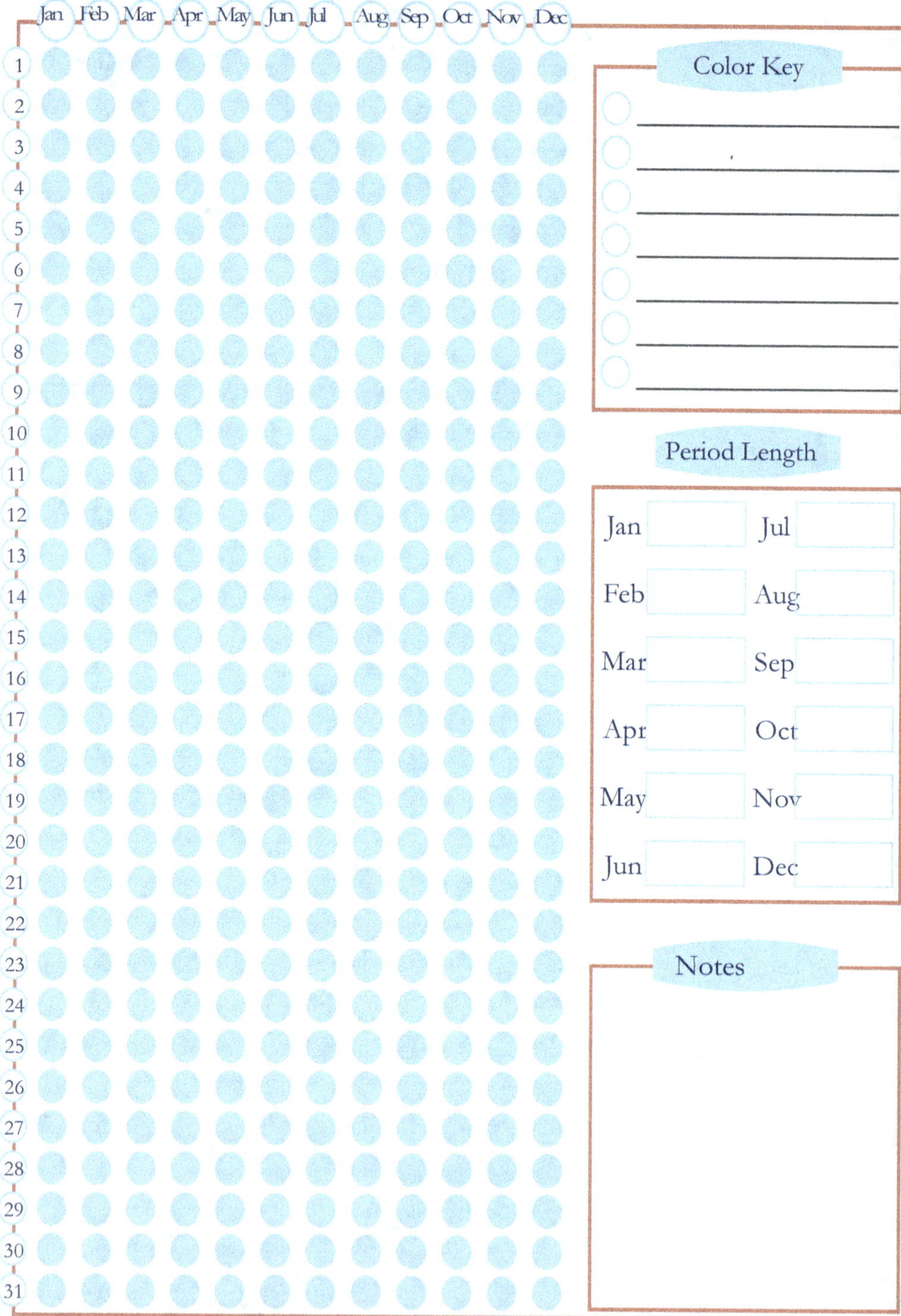

Medication Tracker

Date	✓	Medicine	Time

Medication Tracker

Date	✓	Medicine	Time

Water Tracker

	Week1	Week2	Week3	Week4	Week5	Week6	Week7
Mon							
Tue							
Wed							
Thu							
Fri							
Sat							
Sun							

Notes:

Goals:

Water Tracker

	Week1	Week2	Week3	Week4	Week5	Week6	Week7
Mon							
Tue							
Wed							
Thu							
Fri							
Sat							
Sun							

Notes:

Goals:

Sleep Tracker

Date	Hours												Notes
1	01	02	03	04	05	06	07	08	09	10	11	12	
2	01	02	03	04	05	06	07	08	09	10	11	12	
3	01	02	03	04	05	06	07	08	09	10	11	12	
4	01	02	03	04	05	06	07	08	09	10	11	12	
5	01	02	03	04	05	06	07	08	09	10	11	12	
6	01	02	03	04	05	06	07	08	09	10	11	12	
7	01	02	03	04	05	06	07	08	09	10	11	12	
8	01	02	03	04	05	06	07	08	09	10	11	12	
9	01	02	03	04	05	06	07	08	09	10	11	12	
10	01	02	03	04	05	06	07	08	09	10	11	12	
11	01	02	03	04	05	06	07	08	09	10	11	12	
12	01	02	03	04	05	06	07	08	09	10	11	12	
13	01	02	03	04	05	06	07	08	09	10	11	12	
14	01	02	03	04	05	06	07	08	09	10	11	12	
15	01	02	03	04	05	06	07	08	09	10	11	12	
16	01	02	03	04	05	06	07	08	09	10	11	12	
17	01	02	03	04	05	06	07	08	09	10	11	12	
18	01	02	03	04	05	06	07	08	09	10	11	12	
19	01	02	03	04	05	06	07	08	09	10	11	12	
20	01	02	03	04	05	06	07	08	09	10	11	12	
21	01	02	03	04	05	06	07	08	09	10	11	12	
22	01	02	03	04	05	06	07	08	09	10	11	12	
23	01	02	03	04	05	06	07	08	09	10	11	12	
24	01	02	03	04	05	06	07	08	09	10	11	12	
25	01	02	03	04	05	06	07	08	09	10	11	12	
26	01	02	03	04	05	06	07	08	09	10	11	12	
27	01	02	03	04	05	06	07	08	09	10	11	12	
28	01	02	03	04	05	06	07	08	09	10	11	12	
29	01	02	03	04	05	06	07	08	09	10	11	12	
30	01	02	03	04	05	06	07	08	09	10	11	12	
31	01	02	03	04	05	06	07	08	09	10	11	12	

Sleep Tracker

Date	Hours												Notes
1	01	02	03	04	05	06	07	08	09	10	11	12	
2	01	02	03	04	05	06	07	08	09	10	11	12	
3	01	02	03	04	05	06	07	08	09	10	11	12	
4	01	02	03	04	05	06	07	08	09	10	11	12	
5	01	02	03	04	05	06	07	08	09	10	11	12	
6	01	02	03	04	05	06	07	08	09	10	11	12	
7	01	02	03	04	05	06	07	08	09	10	11	12	
8	01	02	03	04	05	06	07	08	09	10	11	12	
9	01	02	03	04	05	06	07	08	09	10	11	12	
10	01	02	03	04	05	06	07	08	09	10	11	12	
11	01	02	03	04	05	06	07	08	09	10	11	12	
12	01	02	03	04	05	06	07	08	09	10	11	12	
13	01	02	03	04	05	06	07	08	09	10	11	12	
14	01	02	03	04	05	06	07	08	09	10	11	12	
15	01	02	03	04	05	06	07	08	09	10	11	12	
16	01	02	03	04	05	06	07	08	09	10	11	12	
17	01	02	03	04	05	06	07	08	09	10	11	12	
18	01	02	03	04	05	06	07	08	09	10	11	12	
19	01	02	03	04	05	06	07	08	09	10	11	12	
20	01	02	03	04	05	06	07	08	09	10	11	12	
21	01	02	03	04	05	06	07	08	09	10	11	12	
22	01	02	03	04	05	06	07	08	09	10	11	12	
23	01	02	03	04	05	06	07	08	09	10	11	12	
24	01	02	03	04	05	06	07	08	09	10	11	12	
25	01	02	03	04	05	06	07	08	09	10	11	12	
26	01	02	03	04	05	06	07	08	09	10	11	12	
27	01	02	03	04	05	06	07	08	09	10	11	12	
28	01	02	03	04	05	06	07	08	09	10	11	12	
29	01	02	03	04	05	06	07	08	09	10	11	12	
30	01	02	03	04	05	06	07	08	09	10	11	12	
31	01	02	03	04	05	06	07	08	09	10	11	12	

Habit Tracker

Month

Habits

M T W T F S S

Habit Tracker

Month

Habits

M T W T F S S

CHALLENGE AUTOMATIC NEGATIVE THOUGHTS WORKSHEET

1 RECOGNIZE & ISOLATE THOUGHT

Building awareness allows you an opportunity to challenge and refute those negative thoughts

1. Stop and pause for a moment, recognize what you are thinking isn't quite right
2. Pay attention to your body and emotions
3. Isolate and focus on the irrational thought and try to separate it from who you are
4. Think about what you are thinking about by having an external view of your thought

2 WRITE DOWN YOUR THOUGHT

Focus and think about what the thought is really about and write it out. After writing, you will feel a sense of relief that your mind has been emptied.

3 DISTRESS LEVEL

Identify the distress level (0-10):

0 = Calm   10 = Extreme

4 DISTORTION TYPE

Identify the cognitive distortion:

(Refer to list of cognitive distortions)

5 CHALLENGE & REFRAME THOUGHT

Challenge the cognitive distortion by evaluating evidence, focusing on positives, and avoid thinking in extremes (Refer to list of challenges):

1. Challenge & refute negative thoughts
2. Modify language and internal dialogue
3. Replace negative distortions with positive healthy thoughts
4. Write down the more reasonable reframed thought

6 REEVALUATE DISTRESS LEVEL

Reevaluate the distress level (0-10) and compare it to step 3. If the distress level has not decreased, consider repeating the exercise again.

GET YOUR DAILY HAPPINESS CHEMICALS

The happy brain chemicals that make you feel good

DOPAMINE

- Enables motivation, learning, and pleasure
- Gives you determination to accomplish goals, desires, and needs

OXYTOCIN

- Feeling of trust, motivates you to build and sustain relationships
- Known as "Cuddle or Love Hormone", plays a role in bonding

SEROTONIN

- Feeling significant or important among peers
- Calm form of accepting yourself with the people around you

ENDORPHINS

- Releases a brief euphoria to mask physical pain
- Response to pain and stress that alleviates anxiety and depression

2 How Deficiency Affects You

DOPAMINE	OXYTOCIN	SEROTONIN	ENDORPHINS
• procrastination • low self-esteem • lack of motivation • low energy or fatigue • inability to focus • feeling anxious • feeling hopeless • mood swings	• feeling lonely • stressed • lack of motivation • low energy or fatigue • disconnect of relationships • feeling anxious • insomnia	• low self-esteem • overly sensitive • anxiety/panic attacks • mood swings • feeling hopeless • social phobia • obsession/compulsion • insomnia	• anxiety • depression • mood swings • aches and pains • insomnia • impulsive behavior

3 How to Increase Happiness Levels

DOPAMINE	OXYTOCIN	SEROTONIN	ENDORPHINS
• meditate • daily to-do list • long term goals • food rich in L-Tyrosine • exercise regularly • create something: writing, music, or art	• physical touch • socializing • massage • acupuncture • listening to music • exercise • cold shower • meditate	• exercise • cold showers • sunlight • massage	• laughter/crying • creating music/art • eat dark chocolate • eat spicy foods • exercise/stretching • massage • meditate

OVERSTIMULATION OF HAPPINESS

Prevent overstimulation and increase the effects of happiness chemicals

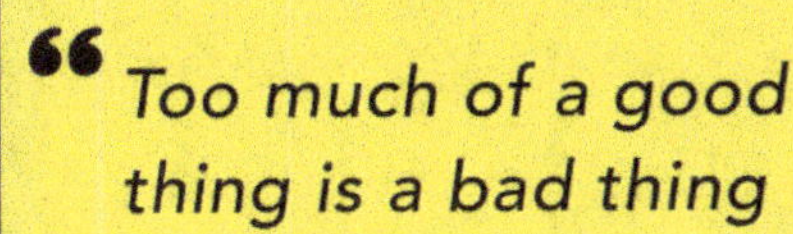

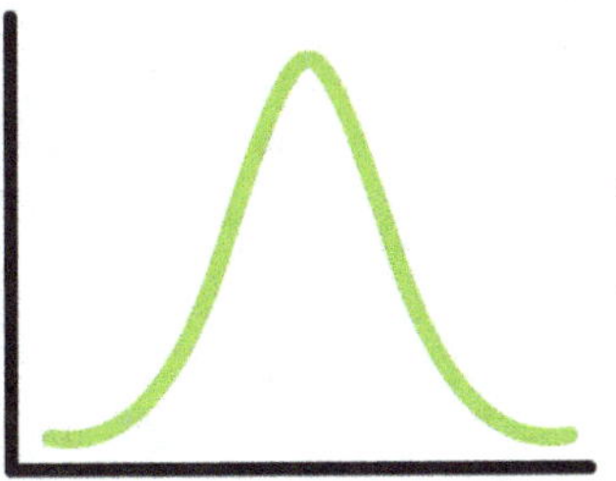

NORMAL

A short spike of happiness effects with a quick drop back to a normal state after the experience is over.

OVERSTIMULATION LEADS TO:

- desensitization of happiness effects
- tolerance to the amount you receive
- addiction towards the activity

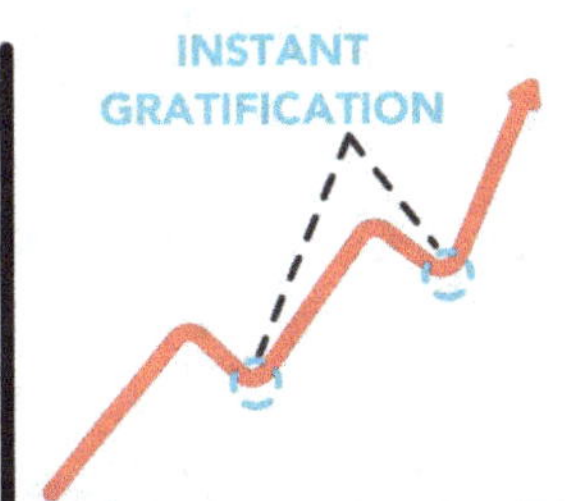

SUPERNORMAL STIMULI

You're continually feeding yourself overstimulating activities and not allowing levels to drop to a normal state.

COMMON OVERSTIMULATING ACTIVITIES:

- scrolling through social media
- always eating fast food
- binge-watching a tv show all weekend

Prevent Overstimulation

Allow levels of happiness chemicals to drop to a normal level to help maintain sensitization.

1. Limiting Your Use by Stopping After Some Time
2. Limiting the Frequency of Use
3. Not Using it Like a Drug
4. Not Using it as an Escape Mechanism

Increase Happiness Receptors

Overstimulation causes receptors to be destroyed, which leads to desensitization.

1. Abstaining from Overstimulating Activities
2. High-Intensity Interval Training
3. Digital Detox
4. Cold Showers or Ice Baths

Post Therapy Notes

Post Therapy Notes